INTRODUCTION
TO POSITIVE
PHILOSOPHY

ISBN 0-87220-050-7 paperback
(formerly 0-672-60284-9)

INTRODUCTION TO POSITIVE PHILOSOPHY

AUGUSTE COMTE

*Edited, with introduction
and revised translation, by*
FREDERICK FERRÉ

Hackett Publishing Company, Inc.
Indianapolis / Cambridge

4 5 6

Library of Congress Cataloging-in-Publication Data
Comte, Auguste, 1798-1857.
    [Cours de philosophie positive. English. Selections]
    Introduction to positive philosophy / Auguste Comte; edited, with
introduction and revised translation, by Frederick Ferré.
        p.   cm.
    This book represents a translation of the first two chapters of the
first volume of the author's Cours de philosophie positive.
    Originally published: Indianapolis: Bobbs-Merrill, 1970.
    Bibliography: p.
    Includes index.
    ISBN 0-87220-051-5   ISBN 0-87220-050-7 (pbk.)
    1. Positivism.   I. Ferré, Frederick.   II. Title.
B2223.E5C55 1988
146'.4 — dc 19   87-34831
                                                                    CIP

CONTENTS

INTRODUCTION

I

The stormy, creative life of the founder of positivist philosophy began in the year 1798, when all of France was racked and torn from the recent excesses of its great Revolution. Born into a devout Roman Catholic and royalist-sympathizing family, the boy christened Isidore Auguste Marie François Xavier Comte was soon to repudiate his background and to become one of the radical thinkers of modern times.

By the age of fourteen Comte had abandoned all belief in God, to which (even in his highly religious later years) he never returned. About the same time he announced himself politically in the anti-royalist, republican camp, and applied for admission to the *École Polytechnique* in hopes of receiving a first-rate scientific education. At first he was rejected because of his youth, despite having scored highest of all applicants on the entrance examination, but by 1814 he was allowed to enroll in this justly famed technical institute where he was to know rare contentment for a time.

This time was cut short, however, by a shift in France's variable political winds, and Comte—together with the entire student body—was expelled for radicalism in 1816. Alienated from his bewildered family and without formal student status, the eighteen-year-old Comte would not admit defeat and soon set to work supporting himself by tutoring in mathematics while continuing a voracious program of general reading.

His brilliance and energy were not long overlooked. In the next year, 1817, the young Comte was appointed secretary to the outstanding social theorist, Saint-Simon, who, forty years his elder, was then at the crest of his fame and influence. This seven-year period as an intellectual intimate to Saint-Simon, though it ended acrimoniously, was vastly important to Comte's self-education and to his developing views. Saint-Simon, for example, had already enunciated a theory of historical development akin to Comte's famous Law of the Three Stages; but even apart from specific theories, a general outlook on man and society was imbibed by the youthful secretary, even as he grew increasingly unhappy about Saint-Simon's weakness in technical rigor and what Comte saw as a scandalous disregard for scientific-empirical modes of argument.

By 1824 the breach (involving personal as well as philosophic differences) was complete, and Comte again found himself on his own. But now, at the age of 26, he felt ready to begin the formulation of his own comprehensive views as he set out once more to make a living as an intellectual odd-job man. After two years, within which period he married, Comte was ready to make a preliminary statement of his systematic reflections in the form of a series of lectures comprising a "course" in the positive philosophy he had been shaping. These lectures, begun in 1826, were informal; that is, they were not sponsored by any academic institution, but they drew a number of eminent scientists and other intellectuals into Comte's small audience. Unfortunately, a long postponement was required after the third lecture, due to a mental breakdown suffered by the always delicately balanced Comte, but by 1829 the *cours* was resumed and completed just as initially planned.

Promptly in 1830 the first volume of the published version of this *cours* appeared (from which the selections in this book are drawn), and gradually over the years the entire six-volume

Cours de philosophie positive came from the press, complete at last in 1842.

In the same year Comte, now 44 years old, finally ended his persistently unhappy marriage—a marriage he blamed for delaying the completion of his published *Cours*. Two years later, however, Comte fell deeply in love with another woman, Madame Clothilde de Vaux, in a way that changed his entire life and added a new dimension to his thought. Clothilde, who had been victimized and deserted by her husband, returned friendly affection to Comte but refused him her bed, for which Comte (previously by no means accustomed to such chastity) eventually thanked her with moving sincerity. His life was permanently changed. Even Clothilde's early death at 31 years of age in 1846 (Comte then being 48) left him eagerly devoted to her memory and raptly dedicated to a life centered in the high love she represented to him.

This personal upheaval influenced the second, concluding, part of Comte's intellectual project. His first effort had been to work out a synoptic account of all the cognitive domains. Here he intended not only to put theology, metaphysics, and science in their proper places but also to analyze in a unified way the relationship among the basic sciences themselves. The second great aim, apparently foreseen quite clearly from the start, was to examine the implications of such a cognitive revolution for human civilization. What kinds of political, what sorts of religious, consequences would flow from the basic changes that a positivist philosophy would bring about? To these questions Comte turned next in a series of works, the primary one of which appeared in four volumes between 1851 and 1854 under the title *Système de politique positive*. His fundamental recommendation in this latter phase of his work, in the four-volume *Système* as well as in the *Catéchisme positiviste* (1852) and the final, fragmentary *La Synthèse subjective* (1856), was that men recognize their legitimate need for religion but fill this need without resorting to supernaturalism or to the violation of intellectual integrity. Intelligence and sensitivity, rigor and responsibility can, Comte argued, be synthesized in a humanistic religion that combines truth, beauty, and goodness through unconditional commitment to "living for others" in gentleness and love.

Comte, unlike some of his rationalist predecessors, did not disregard the legitimate role of ritual in human life, and (in keeping with some of the other religious experimentation of his day in France) proposed for regular veneration a calendar of positivist heroes to replace the saints of the Christian calendar; he even set aside regular periods in his own life for solemn reaffirmation of his enduring love for Clothilde and—more generally—of his devotion to the values that she had come to represent. With much obvious justification he interpreted such solemn acts of meditation to be a humanist's proper method of prayer, and such symbolic acts of rededication to basic values to be a naturalist's avenue to the refreshments of genuine worship.

In 1857, not yet 60 years old and in the midst of the second volume of *La Synthèse subjective*, Comte's health finally broke. His conservative enemies in the intellectual "establishment" had retaliated for his philosophic criticisms with economic weapons, and for a considerable period in his life he was kept narrowly from destitution only by a subscription raised for him through the organizing efforts of John Stuart Mill. But despite his personal exhaustion, poverty, and relative isolation at the time of his death, Auguste Comte's legacy of thought has been a rich one, stimulating some followers to almost cultic passion and leaving all of us who try to think in the modern world measurably in his debt.

II

This little book represents the first two chapters of the first volume of Comte's great *Cours de philosophie positive*. In these introductory chapters Comte succinctly outlined his fundamental aims, methods, and theses for the entire six-volume work. As such, they represent what is perhaps the best first-hand exposition of classical positivism ever offered by its founder in a convenient form. Quite obviously, these chapters will not take the place of the multi-volume work they originally served to preface, but, equally clearly, they do not depend for their philosophic usefulness upon the massive marshaling of data—much of it redundant or now obsolete—that is found in the remainder of the *Cours*.

This is not, indeed, the first time that this key material has been published separately. Besides an early edition in French, an English translation of these two chapters of the *Cours* was published in 1905 by Watts and Company, and it is upon this translation by Paul Descours (Chapter One) and H. Gordon Jones (Chapter Two) that the present edition is based.

The passage of more than a half century since the previous translation, however, called for a fresh comparison of the Watts edition with the original French, and revision at a great many points. In this process I was greatly aided both by the linguistic sensitivity and by the philosophic acuteness of my colleague Michel de Repentigny, who discussed every line of this edition with me in terms of Comte's own native manner of expression. That manner, it should be noted, is not always as felicitous as a translator or an editor might wish. To some extent I have attempted to smooth out style in the process of revising the 1905 translation, but I have restrained myself in most cases when in doubt.*

Certain systematic changes should be noted, however, at least for the record. I have taken the editorial responsibility for turning the material below more definitely into the form of chapters than of written lectures. This process was begun in the 1905 edition but was not carried through completely, sometimes with disconcerting results. I have also dropped, without indicating the elision, Comte's rather frequent references to what he intends to expand or to show at greater length in other parts of his *Cours*. Readers of the present edition should understand that practically every point is dealt with in much greater detail than can be fitted into these two chapters, the function of which is clearly not to be exhaustive. Likewise, when Comte refers to his *Cours* as a

---

* Spelling and punctuation have been changed to conform to American usage.

whole, I have translated such references by phrases such as "this work" rather than "this course." Consequently, the reader of this edition should understand that "this work," when it appears below, has reference to material that extends far beyond the bounds of the two chapters presently in his hands. Perhaps these readers will be lured by such reference to Comte's original mammoth product.

FREDERICK FERRÉ

SELECTED
BIBLIOGRAPHY

WORKS BY COMTE IN ENGLISH TRANSLATION

Comte, Auguste. *The Positive Philosophy*. Freely translated and condensed by Harriet Martineau. 2 vols. London, 1853. New York: Calvin Blanchard, 1855. [Condensed English version of the *Cours de philosophie positive*, 1830–1842.]

———. *A General View of Positivism*. Translated by J. H. Bridges. London: W. Reeves, n.d. New York: Robert Speller & Sons, 1957. [English translation of *Discours sur l'ensemble du positivism*, 1848.]

———. *The System of Positive Polity*. Translated by J. H. Bridges, Frederic Harrison, et al. London, 1875–1877. [English translation of *Système de politique positive*, 1851–1854.]

———. *The Catechism of Positive Religion*. Translated by Richard Congreve. London: Kegan Paul & Co., 1958. [English translation of *Catéchisme positiviste*, 1852.]

WORKS ABOUT COMTE IN ENGLISH

Mill, John Stuart. *Auguste Comte and Positivism*. London, 1865.

Lévy-Bruhl, Lucien. *The Philosophy of Auguste Comte*. Translated by Kathleen de Beaumont-Klein. New York, 1903. [English translation of *La Philosophie d'Auguste Comte*, 1900.]

Whittaker, Thomas. *Comte and Mill*. London, 1908.

Hawkins, Richard Laurin. *Auguste Comte and the United States (1816–1853)*. Cambridge, Massachusetts: Harvard University Press, 1926.

———. *Positivism in the United States (1853–1861)*. Cambridge, Massachusetts: Harvard University Press, 1938.

Simon, W. M. *European Positivism in the Nineteenth Century: An Essay in Intellectual History*. Ithaca, New York: Cornell University Press, 1963.

INTRODUCTION
TO POSITIVE
PHILOSOPHY

I

THE NATURE
AND IMPORTANCE
OF THE POSITIVE
PHILOSOPHY

In order to explain properly the true nature and peculiar character of the positive philosophy, it is indispensable that we should first take a brief survey of the progressive growth of the human mind viewed as a whole; for no idea can be properly understood apart from its history.

In thus studying the total development of human intelligence in its different spheres of activity, from its first and simplest beginning up to our own time, I believe that I have discovered a great fundamental law, to which the mind is subjected by an invariable necessity. The truth of this law can, I think, be demonstrated both by reasoned proofs furnished by a knowledge of our mental organization, and by historical verification due to an attentive study of the past. This law consists in the fact that each of our principal conceptions, each branch of our knowledge, passes in succession through three different theoretical states: the theological or fictitious state, the metaphysical or abstract state, and the scientific or positive state. In other words, the human mind—by its very nature—makes use successively in each of its researches of three methods of philosophizing, whose characters are essentially different and even radically opposed to each other. We have first the theological method, then the metaphysical method, and finally the positive method. Hence, there are three kinds of philosophy or general systems of conceptions on the aggregate of phenomena which are mutually exclusive of each other. The first is the necessary starting point of human intelligence; the third represents its fixed and definitive state; the second is destined to serve only as a transitional method.

In the theological state, the human mind directs its researches mainly toward the inner nature of beings, and toward the first and final causes of all the phenomena that it observes—in a word, toward absolute knowledge. It therefore represents these phenomena as being produced by the direct and continuous action of more or less numerous supernatural agents, whose arbitrary intervention explains all the apparent anomalies of the universe.

In the metaphysical state, which is in reality only a simple general modification of the first state, the supernatural agents are replaced by abstract forces, real entities or personified abstractions, inherent in the different beings of the world. These entities are looked upon as capable of giving rise by themselves to all the phenomena observed, each phenomenon being explained by assigning it to its corresponding entity.

Finally, in the positive state, the human mind, recognizing the impossibility of obtaining absolute truth, gives up the search after the origin and hidden causes of the universe and a knowledge of the final causes of phenomena. It endeavours now only to discover, by a well-combined use of reasoning and observation, the actual laws of phenomena—that is to say, their invariable relations of succession and likeness. The explanation of facts, thus reduced to its real terms, consists henceforth only in the connection established between different particular phenomena and some general facts, the number of which the progress of science tends more and more to diminish.

The theological system arrived at its highest form of perfection when it substituted the providential action of a single being for the varied play of the numerous independent gods which had been imagined by the primitive mind. In the same way, the last stage of the metaphysical system consisted in replacing the different special entities by the idea of a single great general entity—nature—looked upon as the sole source of all phenomena. Similarly, the ideal of the positive system, toward which it constantly tends, although in all probability it will never attain such a stage, would be reached if we could look upon all the different phenomena observable as so many particular cases of a single general fact, such as that of gravitation, for example.

This is not the place to give a special demonstration of this fundamental law of mental development, and to deduce from it its most important consequences. We shall make a direct study of it, with all the necessary details, in the part of this work relating to social phenomena.[1] I am considering it now only in order to determine precisely the true character of the positive philosophy, as opposed to the two other philosophies which have successively dominated our whole intellectual system up to these latter centuries. For the present, to avoid leaving entirely undemonstrated so important a law, the applications of which frequently occur throughout this work, I must confine myself to a rapid enumeration of the most evident general reasons that prove its exactitude.

In the first place, it is, I think, sufficient merely to enunciate such a law for its accuracy to be immediately verified by all those who are fairly well acquainted with the general history of the sciences. For there is not a single science that has today reached the positive stage, which was not in the past—as each can easily see for himself—composed mainly of metaphysical abstractions, and, going back further still, it was altogether under

[1] Readers who desire to have a fuller explanation of this subject, without delay, may consult with advantage three articles entitled "Philosophical Considerations on the Sciences and Men of Science," which I published in November, 1825, in a journal called the *Producteur* (numbers seven, eight, and ten), and especially the first part of my *System of Positive Polity*, addressed in April, 1824, to the Academy of Sciences, where I placed on record for the first time my discovery of this law.
[This note appears in the original text. All other notes have been added by the editor.]

the sway of theological conceptions. Unfortunately, we shall have to recognize on more than one occasion in the different parts of this course, that even the most perfect sciences retain today some very evident traces of these two primitive states.

This general revolution of the human mind can, moreover, be easily verified today in a very obvious, although indirect, manner, if we consider the development of the individual intelligence. The starting point being necessarily the same in the education of the individual as in that of the race, the various principal phases of the former must reproduce the fundamental epochs of the latter. Now, does not each of us in contemplating his own history recollect that he has been successively—as regards the most important ideas—a theologian in childhood, a metaphysician in youth, and a natural philosopher in manhood? This verification of the law can easily be made by all who are on a level with their era.

But in addition to the proofs of the truth of this law furnished by direct observation of the race or the individual, I must, above all, mention in this brief summary the theoretical considerations that show its necessity.

The most important of these considerations arises from the very nature of the subject itself. It consists in the need at every epoch of having some theory to connect the facts, while, on the other hand, it was clearly impossible for the primitive human mind to form theories based on observation.

All competent thinkers agree with Bacon[2] that there can be no real knowledge except that which rests upon observed facts. This fundamental maxim is evidently indisputable if it is applied, as it ought to be, to the mature state of our intelligence. But, if we consider the origin of our knowledge, it is no less certain that the primitive human mind could not and, indeed, ought not to have thought in that way. For if, on the one hand, every positive theory must necessarily be founded upon observations, it is, on

[2] Francis Bacon (1561–1626), English philosopher largely responsible for laying the modern foundations of experimentalism in science and resolute empiricism in philosophy.

the other hand, no less true that, in order to observe, our mind has need of some theory or other. If in contemplating phenomena we did not immediately connect them with some principles, not only would it be impossible for us to combine these isolated observations and, therefore, to derive any profit from them, but we should even be entirely incapable of remembering the facts, which would for the most part remain unnoted by us.

Thus, there were two difficulties to be overcome: the human mind had to observe in order to form real theories; and yet it had to form theories of some sort before it could apply itself to a connected series of observations. The primitive human mind, therefore, found itself involved in a vicious circle, from which it would never have had any means of escaping if a natural way out of the difficulty had not fortunately been found by the spontaneous development of theological conceptions. These presented a rallying point for the efforts of the mind, and furnished materials for its activity. This is the fundamental motive which demonstrates the logical necessity for the purely theological character of primitive philosophy, apart from those important social considerations relating to the matter which I cannot even indicate now.

This necessity becomes still more evident when we regard the perfect congruity of theological philosophy with the peculiar nature of the researches on which the human mind in its infancy concentrated to so high a degree all its efforts. It is, indeed, very noticeable that the most insoluble questions—such as the inner nature of objects, or the origin and purpose of all phenomena—are precisely those which the human mind proposes to itself, in preference to all others, in its primitive state, all really soluble problems being looked upon as hardly worthy of serious thought. The reason for this is very obvious, since it is experience alone that has enabled us to estimate our abilities rightly, and, if man had not commenced by overestimating his forces, these would never have been able to acquire all the development of which they are capable. This fact is a necessity of our organization. But, be that as it may, let us picture to ourselves as far as we are able this [early] mental disposition, so universal and so prominent, and let us ask ourselves what kind of reception would have been accorded at such an epoch to the positive philosophy, supposing it to have been then formed. The highest ambition of this philosophy is to discover the laws of phenomena, and its main characteristic is precisely that of regarding as necessarily interdicted to the human reason all those sublime mysteries which theological philosophy, on the contrary, explains with such admirable facility, even to the smallest detail. [Under such circumstances, it is easy to see what the choice of primitive man would be.]

The same thing is true when we consider from a practical standpoint the nature of the pursuits with which the human mind first occupies itself. Under that aspect they offer to man the strong attraction of an unlimited control over the exterior world, which is regarded as being entirely destined for our use, while all its phenomena seem to have close and continuous relations with our existence. These chimerical hopes, these exaggerated ideas of man's importance in the universe, to which the theological philosophy gives rise, are destroyed irrevocably by the first fruits of the positive philosophy. But at the beginning they afforded an indispensable stimulus without the aid of which we cannot, indeed, conceive how the primitive human mind would have been induced to undertake any arduous labors.

We are at the present time so far removed from that early state of mind—at least as regards the majority of phenomena— that it is difficult for us to appreciate properly the force and necessity of such considerations. Human reason is now so mature that we are able to undertake laborious scientific researches without having in view any extraneous goal capable of strongly exciting the imagination, such as that which the astrologers or alchemists proposed to themselves. Our intellectual activity is sufficiently excited by the mere hope of discovering the laws of phenomena, by the simple desire of verifying or disproving a theory. This, however, could not be the case in the infancy of the human mind. Without the attractive chimeras of astrology, or the powerful deceptions of alchemy, for example, where should we have found the perseverance and ardor necessary for collecting the long series of observations and experiments which later on served as a basis for the first positive theories of these two classes of phenomena?

The need for such a stimulus to our intellectual development was keenly felt long ago by Kepler[3] in the case of astronomy, and has been justly appreciated in our own time by Berthollet[4] in chemistry.

The above considerations show us that, although the positive philosophy represents the true final state of human intelligence—that to which it has always tended more and more—it was nonetheless necessary to employ the theological philosophy at first and during many centuries, both as a method and as furnishing provisional doctrines. Because the theological philosophy was spontaneous in its character, it was the only one possible in the beginning; it was also the only one to offer a sufficient interest to our budding intelligence. It is now very easy to see that, in order to pass from this provisional form of philosophy to the final stage, the human mind was naturally obliged to adopt metaphysical methods and doctrines as a transitional form of philosophy. This last consideration is indispensable in order to complete the general sketch of the great law which I have pointed out.

It is easily seen that our understanding, [which was] compelled to progress by almost insensible steps, could not pass suddenly and without any intermediate stages from theological to positive philosophy. Theology and physics are so profoundly incompatible, their conceptions are so radically opposed in character, that, before giving up the one in order to employ the other exclusively, the human intelligence had to make use of intermediate conceptions, which, being of a hybrid character, were eminently fitted to bring about a gradual transition. That is the

[3] Johann Kepler (1571–1630) German astronomer and mathematician, one of the principal founders of modern astronomy through the mathematical formulation of the laws of planetary motion.

[4] Claude Louis Berthollet (1748–1822) French chemist who, with Antoine Lavoisier (1743–1794) reformed modern chemical nomenclature and thus helped to found the modern science of chemistry.

part played by metaphysical conceptions, and they have no other real use. By substituting, in the study of phenomena, a corresponding inseparable entity for a direct supernatural agency—although at first the former was only held to be an offshoot of the latter—man gradually accustomed himself to consider only the facts themselves. This development was caused by the concepts of metaphysical agents gradually becoming so empty through oversubtle qualification that all right-minded persons considered them to be only the abstract names of the phenomena in question. It is impossible to imagine by what other method our understanding could have passed from frankly supernatural to purely natural considerations, or, in other words, from the theological to the positive régime.

I have thus established, insofar as it is possible without entering into a special discussion, which would be out of place at the present moment, that which I conceive to be the general law of mental development. It will now be easy for us to determine precisely the exact nature of the positive philosophy. To do that is the special object of this chapter.

We have seen that the fundamental character of the positive philosophy is to consider all phenomena as subject to invariable natural laws. The exact discovery of these laws and their reduction to the least possible number constitute the goal of all our efforts; for we regard the search after what are called causes, whether first or final, as absolutely inaccessible and unmeaning. It is unnecessary to dwell much on a principle that has now become so familiar to all who have made anything like a serious study of the observational sciences. Everybody, indeed, knows that in our positive explanations, even when they are most complete, we do not pretend to explain the real causes of phenomena, as this would merely throw the difficulty further back; we try only to analyze correctly the circumstances of their production, and to connect them by normal relations of succession and similarity.

Thus, to cite the best example, we say that the general phenomena of the universe are explained—as far as they can be—by the Newtonian law of gravitation. On the one hand, this admirable theory shows us all the immense variety of astronomical facts as only a single fact looked at from different points of view, that fact being the constant tendency of all molecules towards each other in direct proportion to their masses and inversely as the squares of their distances. On the other hand, this general fact is shown to be the simple extension of an extremely familiar and, therefore, well-known phenomenon—the weight of a body at the earth's surface. As to determining what attraction and weight are in themselves, or what their causes are—these are questions which we regard as insoluble and outside the domain of the positive philosophy; we, therefore, rightly abandon them to the imagination of the theologians or the subtleties of the metaphysicians. That it is clearly impossible to solve such questions is shown by the fact that, whenever an attempt has been made to give a rational explanation of the matter, the greatest thinkers have only been able to define one of these principles by the other. Attraction is defined as nothing but universal weight, and weight is said to consist simply in terrestrial attraction. Explanations of this kind raise a smile, if put forward as furnishing us with a knowledge of "things-in-themselves" and the mode of causation of phenomena. They are, however, the only satisfactory results obtainable, for they present as identical two orders of phenomena which for so long a time were regarded as unconnected. No sensible person would nowadays seek to go beyond this.

It would be easy to multiply these examples, which will occur very frequently throughout this treatise, for at the present day all great intellectual operations are conducted in this spirit. To take a single example of this from contemporary works, I will choose the fine series of researches made by Fourier[5] on the theory of heat. This affords us an excellent verification of the preceding general remarks. In this work, the philosophical character of which is so eminently positive, the most important and most precise laws of thermal phenomena are disclosed; but the

[5] Jean Baptiste Joseph Fourier (1768–1830), French mathematician and physicist. Probably in the private audience to which these remarks were first addressed.

author has not once inquired into the intimate nature of heat itself, nor has he mentioned, except to point out its uselessness, the vigorous controversy between the partisans of heat as a material substance and those who make it consist in the vibrations of a universal ether. Yet, that work treats of the most important questions, several of which had never been raised—a clear proof that the human mind, by simply confining itself to researches of an entirely positive order, can find therein inexhaustible food for its highest form of activity without attacking inaccessible problems.

Having thus indicated, insofar as it was possible in this general sketch, the spirit of the positive philosophy, which the whole of this course is intended to develop, we must next consider what stage in the formation of that philosophy has now been reached and what remains to be done in order to constitute it fully.

For this purpose, we must in the first place remember that the different branches of our knowledge were not able to pass at the same rate through the three great phases of their development indicated above, and that consequently they did not arrive simultaneously at the positive state. There exists in this respect an invariable and necessary order that our various classes of conceptions have followed, and were bound to follow, in their progressive course; and the exact consideration of this order is the indispensable complement of the fundamental mental law previously enunciated. That order will form the special subject of the next chapter. At present it is sufficient to know that it conforms to the diverse nature of the phenomena, and that it is determined by their degree of generality, of simplicity, and of reciprocal independence—three considerations which, although quite distinct, lead to the same result. Thus, astronomical phenomena, being the most general, the simplest, and the most independent of all others, were the first to be subjected to positive theories; then followed in succession and for the same reasons the phenomena of terrestrial physics, properly so called, those of chemistry, and, finally, those of physiology.

It is impossible to fix the precise date of this mental revolution; we can say only that, like all other great human events, it took place continuously and at an increasing rate, especially since the labors of Aristotle and the Alexandrian school, and afterward from the introduction of natural science into the west of Europe by the Arabs. However, as it is better to fix an epoch in order to give greater precision to our ideas, I would select that of the great movement imparted to the human intellect two centuries ago by the combined influence of the precepts of Bacon,[6] the conceptions of Descartes,[7] and the discoveries of Galileo.[8] It was then that the spirit of the positive philosophy began to assert itself in the world, in evident opposition to the theological and metaphysical spirit; for it was then that positive conceptions disengaged themselves clearly from the superstitious and scholastic alloy, which had more or less disguised the true character of all the previous scientific work.

Since that memorable epoch, the increasing influence of the positive philosophy and the decadent movement of theological and metaphysical philosophy have been extremely marked. These movements have at last become so pronounced that at the present day it is impossible for any observer acquainted with the spirit of his age to fail to recognize the final bent of the human mind toward positive studies, and the irrevocable break henceforth from those fruitless doctrines and provisional methods that were suited only to its first flight. This fundamental mental revolution will, therefore, necessarily be carried out to the fullest extent. If, then, there still remains some great conquest to be made, some important division of the intellectual domain to be invaded, we can be certain that the transformation will take place there also,

[6] See page 4, note 2.

[7] René Descartes (1596–1650), French philosopher and mathematician, largely responsible for shaping the problems of modern philosophy and for emphasizing the rational, mathematical, and theoretical aspects of science and philosophy.

[8] Galileo Galilei (1564–1642), Italian physicist and astronomer, whose combination of inductive with deductive ways of thinking (uniting Bacon and Descartes, as it were) founded the methodology of modern science, and whose discoveries in various fields provided tremendous impetus to early modern science.

as it has been carried out in all the other branches of science. It would evidently be absurd to suppose that the human mind, which is so disposed to unity of method, would yet preserve indefinitely, in the case of a single class of phenomena, its primitive mode of philosophizing, when it has once adopted for the other classes a new philosophic path of an entirely opposite character.

The whole thing reduces itself, therefore, to a simple question of fact: Does the positive philosophy, which during the last two centuries has gradually acquired so great an extension, embrace at the present day all classes of phenomena? It is evident that it does not; therefore, a great scientific work still remains to be executed in order to give the positive philosophy that universal character indispensable for its final constitution.

In the four principal categories of natural phenomena enumerated above—astronomical, physical, chemical, and physiological—we notice an important omission relating to social phenomena. Although these are implicitly comprised among physiological phenomena, yet, owing to their importance and the inherent difficulties of their study, they deserve to form a distinct class. This last order of ideas is concerned with the most special, most complicated, and most dependent of all phenomena; it has, therefore, necessarily progressed more slowly than all the preceding orders, even if we do not take into account the more special obstacles to its study which we shall consider later on. However that may be, it is evident that it has not yet been included within the domain of positive philosophy. Theological and metaphysical methods are never used now by anyone in dealing with all the other kinds of phenomena, either as a means of investigation or even as a mode of reasoning. But these discarded methods are, on the contrary, still used exclusively for both purposes in everything that concerns social phenomena, although their insufficiency in this respect has been fully felt already by all good minds, such men being tired of these empty and endless discussions between, e.g., divine right and the sovereignty of the people.

Here, then, is the great, but evidently the only, gap that has to be filled in order to finish the construction of the positive philosophy. Now that the human mind has founded celestial physics, terrestrial physics (mechanical and chemical), and organic physics (vegetable and animal), it only remains to complete the system of observational sciences by the foundation of social physics.[9] This is at the present time, under several important aspects, the greatest and most pressing of our cognitive needs, and to meet this need is, I make bold to say, the first purpose of this work, its special object.

The conceptions which I shall endeavor to present relating to the study of social phenomena, and of which I hope the present chapter has already enabled us to see the germ, cannot be expected to raise social physics at once to the degree of perfection that has been reached by the earlier branches of natural philosophy. Such a hope would be evidently chimerical, seeing that these branches still differ widely from one another in perfectness, as was, indeed, inevitable. But I aim at impressing upon this last branch of our knowledge the same positive character that already marks all the other branches. If this condition is once really fulfilled, the philosophical system of the modern world will be founded at last in its entirety; for there is no observable fact that would not then be included in one or another of the five great categories of astronomical, physical, chemical, physiological, and social phenomena. All our fundamental conceptions having thus been rendered homogeneous, philosophy will be constituted finally in the positive state. Its character will be henceforth unchangeable, and it will then have only to develop itself indefinitely, by incorporating the constantly increasing knowledge that inevitably results from new observations or more profound meditations. Having by this means acquired the character of universality which as yet it lacks, the positive phi-

---

[9] Comte invented the term "sociology," meant to designate the rigorous study of social phenomena according to the precepts of positive philosophy. But since here Comte is clearly attempting to show the parallels between the various fields of science, his expression "social physics" will be retained.

losophy, with all its natural superiority, will be able to displace entirely the theological and metaphysical philosophies. The only real property possessed by theology and metaphysics at the present day is their character of universality, and when deprived of this motive for preference they will have for our successors only a historical interest.

The first and special object of this course having been thus set forth, it is easy to comprehend its second and general aim, that which constitutes it a course of positive philosophy, and not merely a course on social physics.

The formation of social physics at last completes the system of natural sciences. It, therefore, becomes possible and even necessary to summarize these different sciences, so that they may be coordinated by presenting them as so many branches of a single trunk, instead of continuing to look upon them as only so many isolated groups. Therefore, before proceeding to the study of social phenomena, I shall successively consider, in the encyclopedic order given above, the different positive sciences already formed.

It is, I think, unnecessary to warn the reader that I do not claim to give here a series of special courses of lectures on each of the principal branches of natural philosophy. Not to speak of the enormous time that such an enterprise would take, it is clear that I cannot claim to be equipped for it, nor, I think I may add, can anyone else in the present state of human education. On the contrary, a course of the kind contemplated here requires, if it is to be understood properly, a previous series of special studies on the different sciences which will be treated therein. In the absence of this condition, it is very difficult to realize, and impossible to estimate, the philosophical reflections that will be made upon these sciences. In one word, it is a course on positive philosophy, and not on the positive sciences, that I propose to give. We shall have to consider here only each fundamental science in its relations with the whole positive system and the spirit characterizing it; that is to say, under the twofold aspect of its essential methods and its principal achievements. As to the achievements, indeed, I shall often do no more than mention them as known to specialists, though I shall try to estimate their importance.

In order to sum up the ideas relating to the twofold purpose of this course, I must call attention to the two objects—the one special, the other general—that I have in view and that, although distinct in themselves, are necessarily inseparable. On the one hand, it would be impossible to conceive of a course of positive philosophy unless social physics had been founded first, since an essential element would then be lacking; consequently, the conceptions of such a course would not have that character of generality that ought to be their principal attribute and that distinguishes our present study from any series of special studies. On the other hand, how can we proceed with sure step to the positive study of social phenomena if the mind has not been prepared first by the thorough consideration of positive methods in the case of less complex phenomena, and furnished in addition with a knowledge of the principal laws of earlier phenomena, all of which have a more or less direct influence upon social facts?

Although all the fundamental sciences do not inspire ordinary minds with an equal interest, there is not one of them that should be neglected in such a study as we are about to undertake. As regards the welfare of the human race, all of them are certainly of equal importance when we examine them thoroughly. Besides, those whose results seem at first sight to offer only a minor practical interest are yet of the greatest importance, owing to either the greater perfection of their methods or the indispensable foundation of all the others. This is a consideration to which I shall have special occasion to refer in the next chapter.

To guard as far as possible against the misconceptions likely to arise respecting a work as novel as this, I must add a few remarks to the explanations already given. I refer especially to that universal predominance of specialism, which hasty readers might think was the tendency of this course, and which is so rightly looked upon as wholly contrary to the true spirit of the positive philosophy. These remarks, moreover, will have the more important advantage of exhibiting this spirit under a new aspect, calculated to make its general idea clearer.

In the primitive state of our knowledge, no regular division exists among intellectual labors; all the sciences are cultivated simultaneously by the same minds. This method of organizing human studies is at first inevitable and even indispensable, as I shall have occasion to show later on; but it gradually changes in proportion as the different orders of conceptions develop themselves. By a law whose necessity is evident, each branch of the scientific system gradually separates from the trunk when it has developed far enough to admit of separate cultivation—that is to say, when it has arrived at a stage in which it is capable of constituting the sole pursuit of certain minds. It is to this division of the various kinds of research among different orders of scientists that we evidently owe the development which each distinct class of human knowledge has attained in our time; but this very division renders it impossible for modern scientists to practice that simultaneous cultivation of all the sciences which was so easy and so common in antiquity. In a word, the division of intellectual labor, carried out further and further, is one of the most important and characteristic attributes of the positive philosophy.

But, while recognizing the prodigious results due to this division, and while seeing that it henceforth constitutes the true fundamental basis of the general organization of the scientific world, it is, on the other hand, impossible not to be struck by the great inconveniences which it at present produces, because of the excessive specialization of the ideas that exclusively occupy each mind. This unfortunate result, being inherent in the very principle of the division of labor, is no doubt inevitable up to a certain point. Do what we will, therefore, we shall never be able to equal the ancients in this respect, for their general superiority was due to the slight degree of development of their knowledge. Yet, I think we can, by proper means, avoid the most pernicious effects of an exaggerated specialism without doing injury to the fruitful influence of the division of labor in research. There is an urgent need to consider this question seriously, for these inconveniences, which by their very nature tend constantly to increase, are now becoming very apparent. Everyone agrees that the divisions which we establish between the various branches of natural philosophy, in order to make our labors more perfect, are at bottom artificial. In spite of this admission, we must not forget that the number of scientists who study the whole of even a single science is already very small, although such a science is, in its turn, only a part of a greater whole. The majority of scientists already confine themselves entirely to the isolated consideration of a more or less extensive section of a particular science, without concerning themselves much about the relationship between their special work and the general system of positive knowledge. Let us hasten to remedy this evil before it becomes more serious. Let us take care that the human mind does not lose its way in a mass of detail. We must not conceal from ourselves that this is the essentially weak side of our system, and that this is the point on which the partisans of theological and metaphysical philosophy may still attack the positive philosophy with some hope of success.

The true means of arresting the pernicious influence that seems to threaten the intellectual future of mankind, because of too great a specialization of individual researches, is clearly not to return to the ancient confusion of labors. This would tend to put the human mind back; and, besides, such a return has happily become impossible now. The true remedy consists, on the contrary, in perfecting the division of labor itself. All that is necessary is to create one more great speciality, consisting in the study of general scientific traits. We need a new class of properly trained scientists who, instead of devoting themselves to the special study of any particular branch of science, shall employ themselves solely in the consideration of the different positive sciences in their present state. It would be their function to determine exactly the character of each science, to discover the relations and concatenation of the sciences, and to reduce, if possible, all their chief principles to the smallest number of common principles, while always conforming to the fundamental maxims of the positive method. At the same time the other scientists, before devoting themselves to their respective specialities, should have received a previous training embracing all the general principles of positive knowledge. This would enable them henceforth to make immediate use of the light thrown on their work by the scientists devoted to the study of the sciences in general, whose results the specialists would in turn be able to rectify. That is a state of things to which the existing scientists are drawing nearer every day. If these two great conditions were once fulfilled, as they evidently can be, then the division of labor in the sciences could be carried on without any danger as far as the development of the different kinds of knowledge required. There would be a distinct class of men [always open to the critical discipline of all the other classes], whose special and permanent function would consist in connecting each new special discovery with the general system; and we should then have no cause to fear that too great an attention bestowed upon the details would ever prevent us from perceiving the whole. In a word, the modern organization of the scientific world would then be accomplished, and would be susceptible of indefinite development, while always preserving the same character.

To make the study of the universal characteristics of the sciences a distinct department of intellectual labor is merely a further extension of the same principle of division that led to the successive separation of the different sciences. As long as the different positive sciences were only slightly developed, their mutual relations were not important enough to give rise (at all events permanently) to a special discipline, nor was the need of this new study nearly as urgent as it is now. But at the present day each of the sciences has developed on its own lines to such an extent that the examination of a mutual relationship affords material for systematic and continued labor, while at the same time this new order of studies becomes indispensable to prevent the dispersion of human ideas.

Such, in my view, is the office of the positive philosophy in relation to the positive sciences, properly so called. Such, at all events, is the aim of the present work.

I have now determined, as exactly as possible in a first sketch, the general spirit of a course of positive philosophy. In order to bring out its full character, I must state concisely the principal general advantages that such a work may have—if its essential conditions are fulfilled properly—as regards intellectual progress. I will mention only four. They are fundamental qualities of the positive philosophy.

In the first place, the study of the positive philosophy, by considering the results of the activity of our intellectual faculties, furnishes us with the only really rational means of exhibiting the logical laws of the human mind, which have hitherto been sought by methods so ill calculated to reveal them.

To explain what I mean on this point I must first recall a philosophical conception of the highest importance, set forth by Blainville[10] in the fine introduction to his *Principles of Comparative Anatomy*. According to him, every active being, and especially every living being, may be studied in all its manifestations under two fundamental relations—the static and the dynamic; that is, as fitted to act and as actually acting. It is clear that all the considerations which might be presented will necessarily fall under the one or the other of these heads. Let us apply this luminous fundamental maxim to the study of intellectual functions.

If these functions are regarded from a static point of view, their study can consist only in determining the organic conditions on which they depend; it thus forms an essential part of anatomy and physiology. When considering the question from a dynamic point of view, we have merely to study the actual march of the human intellect, in practice, by examining the procedures used by it in order to acquire a knowledge of the various

[10] Henri Marie Ducrotay de Blainville (1778–1850), French naturalist. Probably in the private audience to which these remarks were first addressed.

sciences; this constitutes essentially the general object of the positive philosophy as I have already defined it in this chapter. In brief, we must look upon all scientific theories as so many great logical facts; and it is only by a thorough observation of these facts that we can rise to the knowledge of logical laws.

These are evidently the only two general methods, complementary to each other, by the use of which we are able to arrive at any really rational ideas concerning intellectual phenomena. We see that in no case is there room for that illusory psychology —the last transformation of theology—the revival of which attempts are being made so vainly at the present day. This theory, while ignoring and discarding the physiological study of our intellectual organs and the observation of the rational methods that actually direct our various scientific researches, claims that it can discover the fundamental laws of the human mind, by contemplating it in itself, without paying any attention to either the causes or the effects of its activity.

The preponderance of the positive philosophy has been growing steadily since Bacon's time. It has today acquired, indirectly, so great a hold over even those minds that are the least familiar with its immense development that the metaphysicians devoted to the study of the intellect could only hope to check the decadence of their pretended science by presenting their doctrines as also being founded upon the observation of facts. In order to do this, they have recently attempted to distinguish, by a very singular subtlety, two kinds of observation of equal importance, the one exterior, the other interior, the latter being devoted solely to the study of intellectual phenomena. To enter into a special discussion of this fundamental sophism would be out of place here. I must be content with indicating the principal consideration which proves clearly that this pretended direct contemplation of the mind by itself is a pure illusion.

It was thought until quite recently that vision was explained by saying that the luminous action of bodies produces on the retina actual images representing exterior forms and colors. To this the physiologists have reasonably objected that, if the luminous impressions produced real images on the retina, we should need another eye to see them. Is not this reasoning still more applicable in the present instance?

It is clear that, by an inevitable necessity, the human mind can observe all phenomena directly, except its own. Otherwise, by whom would the observation be made? As far as moral phenomena are concerned, it may be granted that it is possible for a man to observe the passions that animate him, for the anatomical reason that the organs which are their seat are distinct from those whose functions are devoted to observation. Everyone has had occasion to notice this fact for himself, but such observations would evidently never possess much scientific value. The best way of knowing the passions will always be to observe them from the outside; for a person in any state of extreme passion—that is to say, in precisely the state that it is most essential to examine—would necessarily be incapacitated for observing himself. But in the case of intellectual phenomena, to observe them in this manner while they are taking place is clearly out of the question. The thinking individual cannot cut himself in two—one of the parts reasoning, while the other is looking on. Since in this case the organ observed and the observing organ are identical, how could any observation be made?

The principle of this so-called psychological method is therefore entirely worthless. Besides, consider to what thoroughly contradictory proceedings it immediately leads! On the one hand, you are recommended to isolate yourself as far as possible from the outer world, and you must especially give up all intellectual work; for if you were engaged in making only the simplest calculation, what would become of the interior observation? On the other hand, after having, by means of due precautions, at last attained this perfect state of intellectual slumber, you must then occupy yourself in contemplating the operations that will be taking place in a mind supposed to be blank! Our descendants will no doubt see such pretensions ridiculed on the stage some day.

The results of such a strange procedure are in thorough accordance with the principle. For the last two thousand years metaphysicians have been cultivating psychology in this manner, and yet they have not been able to agree on one single intelligible and sound proposition. They are, even at the present day, divided into a multitude of schools that are incessantly disputing on the first elements of their doctrines. In fact, interior observation gives rise to almost as many divergent opinions as there are so-called observers.

The true scientists—the men devoted to the positive sciences —are still calling in vain on these psychologists to cite a single real discovery, great or small, due to this much-vaunted method. It does not follow that all their labors have been absolutely fruitless as regards the general progress of our knowledge, and we must remember the valuable service that they rendered in sustaining the activity of human intelligence at a time when it could not find a more substantial ailment. But their writings consist largely of that which an illustrious positive philosopher, M. Cuvier,[11] has well called "metaphors mistaken for reasoning." We may safely affirm that any true notions they present have been obtained, not by their pretended method, but by observations on the progress of the human mind—observations to which the development of the sciences has from time to time given birth. And even these ideas, so scanty in number, although proclaimed with so much emphasis, and due only to the unfaithfulness of the psychologists to their pretended methods, are generally either greatly exaggerated or very incomplete, and they are very inferior to the remarks that scientists have already unostentatiously made upon the methods which they employ. It would be easy to cite some striking examples of this, if I did not fear that I should be prolonging the discussion of the point too much: take, for instance, the treatment of the theory of [algebraical] signs [by metaphysicians and geometers respectively].

The considerations relating to logical science which I have just indicated become still more evident when we deal with the art of logic.

[11] Georges L. C. F. D. Cuvier (1769–1832), French naturalist and founder of the science of comparative anatomy. An opponent of the evolutionary theories of Jean Baptiste Lamarck (1744–1829).

For when we want not only to know what the positive method consists in, but also to have such a clear and deep knowledge of it as to be able to use it effectively, we must consider it in action; we must study the various great applications of the method that the human mind has made and already verified. In a word, it is only by a philosophical examination of the sciences that we can attain the desired result. The method does not admit of being studied apart from the researches on which it is employed; or, at all events, it is only a lifeless study, incapable of fertilizing the mind that resorts to it. Looking at it in that abstract way, the only real information that you can give about it amounts to no more than a few general propositions, so vague that they can have no influence on mental habits. When we have thoroughly established as a logical thesis that all our knowledge must be founded upon observation, that we must proceed sometimes from facts to principles, at other times from principles to facts, and some other similar aphorisms, we still know the method far less clearly than he who, even without any philosophical purpose in view, has studied at all completely a single positive science. It is because they have failed to recognize this essential fact that our psychologists have been led to take their reveries for science, in the belief that they understood the positive method because they have read the precepts of Bacon or the discourse of Descartes.

I do not know if, in the future, it will become possible to construct by a priori reasoning a genuine course on method, wholly independent of the philosophical study of the sciences; but I am quite convinced that it cannot be done at present, for the great logical methods cannot yet be explained with sufficient precision apart from their applications. I venture to add, moreover, that, even if such an enterprise could be carried out eventually, which is conceivable, it would nevertheless be only through the study of regular applications of scientific methods that we could succeed in forming a good system of intellectual habits; this is, however, the essential object to be gained by studying method. There is no need to insist further just now on a subject that will recur frequently throughout this work and in regard to which I shall present some new considerations in the next chapter.

The first great direct result of the positive philosophy is then the manifestation by experience of the laws that our intellectual functions follow in their operations and, consequently, a precise knowledge of the general rules that are suitable for our guidance in the investigation of truth.

A second consequence, of no less importance and of much more urgent concern, which must immediately result from the establishment of the positive philosophy as defined in this chapter, is the general recasting of our educational system.

Competent judges are already unanimous in recognizing the necessity of replacing our European education, which is still essentially theological, metaphysical, and literary, by a positive education in accordance with the spirit of our time and adapted to the needs of modern civilization. Various attempts have been made in increasing number during the last hundred years, and especially during recent years, to spread and augment, without ceasing, instruction of a positive kind. Such attempts, which the different European governments have always eagerly encouraged and often initiated, are a sufficient testimony that the spontaneous feeling of this necessity is everywhere growing. But, while supporting these useful enterprises as much as possible, we must not conceal the fact that in the present state of our ideas they are not at all capable of attaining their principal object— namely, the fundamental regeneration of general education. The exclusive speciality, the too rigid isolation, which still characterizes our way of conceiving and of cultivating the sciences, has necessarily a marked influence upon the mode of teaching them. An intelligent person who wishes at the present day to study the principal branches of natural philosophy, in order to acquire a general system of positive ideas, is obliged to study each separate science in the same way and with the same amount of detail as if he wished to become an astronomical or chemical specialist, etc. This renders such an education almost impossible and necessarily very imperfect, even in the case of the most intelligent minds placed in the most favorable circumstances. Such a mode of proceeding would, therefore, be wholly chimerical as regards general education; and yet, an essential requirement of the latter is a complete body of positive conceptions on all the great classes of natural phenomena. It is such a general survey, on a more or less extended scale, which must henceforth constitute, even among the mass of the people, the permanent basis of all human combinations; it must, in short, constitute the mental framework of our descendants. In order that natural philosophy may be able to complete the already partially accomplished regeneration of our intellectual system, it is therefore indispensable that the different sciences of which it is composed—regarding them as the different branches of a single trunk—should first be reduced to what constitutes their essence—that is, to their principal methods and most important results. It is in this way only that the teaching of the sciences can become the basis of a new general and really rational education for our people. Of course, each individual, after receiving this general education, will have to supplement it by such special education as he may require, in which he will study one or other of the special sciences. But the essential consideration which I wish to point out here is that all these special studies, even if all of them were toilsomely compiled, would necessarily be insufficient really to renew our educational system, if they did not rest on the preliminary basis of this general education which is itself the direct result of the positive philosophy as defined in this discourse.

The special study of the general traits of the sciences is not only destined to reorganize education, but it will also contribute to the particular progress of the different positive sciences. This constitutes the third fundamental property that I have to point out.

The divisions that we establish between the sciences, although not arbitrary as some people suppose, are yet essentially artificial. In reality, the subject of all our researches is one; we divide it only so that we may, by separating the difficulties, resolve them more easily. And so it not infrequently happens that these established divisions are a hindrance, and that questions arise which need to be treated by combining the points of view of several sciences. This cannot be done easily when scientists are so addicted to specialization. Hence, the problems are left unsolved for a much longer time than would otherwise be necessary. Such an inconvenience must make itself especially felt in the case of the more essential doctrines of each positive science. Very striking examples of this fact could be cited easily, and I shall carefully call attention to them as they occur in the course of this work.

I could cite a very memorable example of this from the past, in the case of the admirable conception of Descartes relating to analytical geometry. This fundamental discovery, which has changed the aspect of mathematical science and in which we should see the true germ of all the great subsequent progress, is it not simply the result of establishing a closer connection between two sciences that had hitherto been regarded from separate standpoints. But the case will be even more decisive if we consider some questions that are still under discussion.

I will take the case, in chemistry, of the important doctrine of definite proportions. It is certain that the memorable discussion which has been raised in our own time, relating to the fundamental principle of this theory, cannot yet be considered, in spite of appearances, as irrevocably terminated. For this is not, in my opinion, a simple question of chemistry. I venture to assert that, in order to settle the point definitively—that is, to determine whether it is a law of nature that atoms necessarily combine together in fixed proportions—it will be indispensable to unite the chemical with the physiological point of view. This is shown by the fact that, even in the opinion of the illustrious chemists who have most powerfully contributed to the formation of this doctrine, the utmost that can be said is that it is always verified in the composition of inorganic bodies; but it is no less constantly at fault in the case of organic compounds, to which up to the present it seems quite impossible to extend the doctrine. Now, before erecting the theory into a truly fundamental principle, ought not this immense exception to be considered first? Does it not belong to the same general characteristic of all organic bodies, that in none of their phenomena can we make use of invariable numbers? However that may be, an entirely new order of considerations, belonging equally to chemistry and physiology, is evidently necessary in order to decide finally, in some way or other, this great question of natural philosophy.

I think it will be well to consider here a second example of the same kind, which since it relates to a subject of much more limited scope, shows even more conclusively the special importance of the positive philosophy in the solution of questions that need the combination of several sciences. This example, which I also take from chemistry, is the still controverted question as to whether, in the present state of our knowledge, nitrogen should be regarded as an element or a compound. The illustrious Berzelius[12] [differing from almost all living chemists] believes it to be a compound; and his reasons, of a purely chemical nature, successfully balance those of present-day chemists. But what I want particularly to point out is that Berzelius, as he admits himself—and a most instructive admission it is—was greatly influenced by the physiological observation that animals that feed on non-nitrogenous matter contain in their tissues just as much nitrogen as the carnivorous animals. It is therefore quite clear that, in order to decide whether nitrogen is or is not an element, we must necessarily call in the aid of physiology, and combine with chemical considerations, properly so called, a series of new researches on the relationships between the composition of living bodies and the nature of their food.

It would be superfluous now to go on multiplying examples of these complex problems, which can be solved only by the ultimate combination of several sciences that are at present cultivated in a wholly independent manner. Those which I have just

---

[12] Jöns Jakob Berzelius (1779–1848). Swedish chemist, discoverer of several new elements and notable contributor to atomic theory after John Dalton (1766–1844).

cited are sufficient to show in a general way the importance of the function that the positive philosophy will perform in perfecting each of the natural sciences, for it is directly destined to organize in a permanent manner combinations of this kind, which could not be formed suitably without its aid.

I must draw attention to a fourth and last fundamental property of that which I have called the positive philosophy, and which no doubt deserves our notice more than any other property, for it is today the most important one from a practical point of view. We may look upon the positive philosophy as constituting the only solid basis of the social reorganization that must terminate the crisis in which the most civilized nations have found themselves for so long. The last part of this course will be specially devoted to establish and develop this proposition. But the general sketch of my great subject which I have undertaken to give in this chapter would lack one of its most characteristic elements if I failed to call attention here to such an essential consideration.

It may be thought that I am making too ambitious a claim for the positive philosophy. But a few very simple reflections will suffice to justify it.

There is no need to prove to readers of this work that the world is governed and overturned by ideas, or, in other words, that the whole social mechanism rests finally on opinions. They know, above all, that the great political and moral crisis of existing societies is due at bottom to intellectual anarchy. Our gravest evil consists, indeed, in this profound divergence that now exists among all minds, with regard to all the fundamental maxims whose fixity is the first condition of a true social order. As long as individual minds are not unanimously agreed upon a certain number of general ideas capable of forming a common social doctrine, we cannot disguise the fact that the nations will necessarily remain in an essentially revolutionary state, in spite of all the political palliatives that may be adopted. Such a condition of things really admits only of provisional institutions. It is equally certain that, if this general agreement upon first principles can once be obtained, the appropriate institutions will necessarily follow, without giving rise to any grave shock; for the greater part of the disorder will have been already dissipated by the mere fact of the agreement. All those, therefore, who feel the importance of a truly normal state of things should direct their attention mainly to this point.

And now, from the lofty standpoint to which the various considerations indicated in this chapter have step by step raised us, it is easy both to characterize clearly the present state of society as regards its inner spirit, and to deduce therefrom the means by which that state can be changed essentially. Returning to the fundamental law enunciated at the commencement of this chapter, I think we may sum up exactly all the observations relating to the existing situation of society, by the simple statement that the actual confusion of men's minds is at bottom due to the simultaneous employment of three radically incompatible philosophies—the theological, the metaphysical, and the positive. It is quite clear that, if any one of these three philosophies really obtained a complete and universal preponderance, a fixed social order would result, whereas the existing evil consists above all in the absence of any true organization. It is the existence of these three opposite philosophies that absolutely prevents all agreement on any essential point. Now, if this opinion be correct, all that is necessary is to know which of the three philosophies can and must prevail by the nature of things; every sensible man should next endeavor to work for the triumph of that philosophy, whatever his particular opinions may have been before the question was analyzed. The question being once reduced to these simple terms, the issue cannot long remain doubtful, because it is evident for all kinds of reasons, some of the principal of which have been indicated in this chapter, that the positive philosophy is alone destined to prevail in the ordinary course of things. It alone has been making constant progress for many centuries, while its antagonists have been as constantly in a state of decay. Whether this is a good or a bad thing matters little; the general fact cannot be denied, and that is sufficient. We may deplore the fact, but we are unable to destroy it; nor, consequently, can we neglect it, on pain of giving ourselves up to illusory speculations. This general revolution of the human mind is at the present time almost entirely accomplished. Nothing more remains to be done, as I have already explained, than to complete the positive philosophy by including in it the study of social phenomena, and then to sum them up in a single body of homogeneous doctrine. When these two tasks have made sufficient progress, the final triumph of the positive philosophy will take place spontaneously, and will reestablish order in society. The marked preference which almost all minds, from the highest to the lowest, show at the present day for positive knowledge, as contrasted with vague and mystical conceptions, augers well for the reception that awaits this philosophy when it shall have acquired the only quality that it still lacks—a character of suitable generality.

To sum up the matter: the theological and metaphysical philosophies are now disputing with each other the task of reorganizing society, although the task is really too hard for their united efforts; it is between these schools only that any struggle still exists in this respect. The positive philosophy has, up to the present, intervened in the contest only in order to criticize both schools; and it has accomplished this task so well as to discredit them entirely. Let us put it in a condition to play an active part, without paying any further attention to debates that have become useless. We must complete the vast intellectual operation commenced by Bacon, Descartes, and Galileo, by furnishing the positive philosophy with the system of general ideas that is destined to prevail henceforth, and for an indefinite future, among the human race. The revolutionary crisis which harasses civilized peoples will then be at an end.

Such are the four principal advantages that will follow from the establishment of the positive philosophy. I have thought it well to mention them at once, because they supplement the general definition that I have tried to give of it.

Before concluding, I desire to caution the reader briefly against an erroneous anticipation which he might form as to the nature of the present work.

In saying that the aim of the positive philosophy was to sum up, in a single body of homogeneous doctrine, the aggregate of acquired knowledge relating to the different orders of natural phenomena, I did not mean that we should proceed to the general study of these phenomena by looking upon them all as so many different effects of a single principle, as reducible to one sole law. Although I must treat this question specially in the next chapter, I think it necessary to say so much at once, in order to avoid unfounded objections that might otherwise be raised. I refer to those critics who might jump to the conclusion that this course is one of those attempts at universal explanation by a single law, which one sees made daily by men who are entire strangers to scientific methods and knowledge. Nothing of that kind is intended here; and the development of this course will furnish the best proof of it to all those whom the explanations contained in this chapter might have left in any doubt on the subject.

It is my deep personal conviction that these attempts at the universal explanation of all phenomena by a single law are highly chimerical, even when they are made by the most competent minds. I believe that the resources of the human mind are too feeble, and the universe is too complicated, to admit of our ever attaining such scientific perfection; and I also think that a very exaggerated idea is generally formed of the advantages to be derived from it, even were it attainable. In any case, it seems to me evident that, considering the present state of our knowledge, we are yet a long way from the time when any such attempt might reasonably be expected to succeed. It seems to me that we could hope to arrive at it only by connecting all natural phenomena with the most general positive law with which we are acquainted—the law of gravitation—which already links all astronomical phenomena to some of the phenomena of terrestrial physics. Laplace[13] has effectively brought forward a conception

---

[13] Pierre Simon Laplace (1749–1827), French astronomer and mathematician, author of *Mécanique céleste* (1799–1825) and particularly noted for his conviction that all the phenomena of the universe can in principle be explained and predicted in terms of the laws of classical mechanics alone.

by which chemical phenomena would be regarded as purely simple molecular effects of Newtonian attraction, modified by the figure and mutual position of the atoms. This conception would probably always remain an open question, owing to the absence of any essential data respecting the intimate constitution of bodies; and it is almost certain that the difficulty of applying the idea would be so great that we should still be obliged to retain, as an artificial aid, the division which at present is regarded as natural between astronomy and chemistry. Accordingly, Laplace only presented this idea as a mere philosophical game which is incapable of really exercising any useful influence on the progress of chemical science. The case is really stronger, however, for even if we supposed this insurmountable difficulty overcome, we should still not have attained scientific unity, since it would be necessary next to connect the same law of gravitation with the whole of physiology; and this would certainly not be the least difficult part of the task. Yet, the hypothesis which we have just been discussing would be, on the whole, the most favorable to this much-desired unity.

I have no need to go further into details in order to convince the reader that the object of this course is by no means to present all natural phenomena as being at bottom identical, apart from the variety of circumstances. The positive philosophy would no doubt be more perfect if this were possible. But this condition is not at all necessary, either for its systematic formation or for the realization of the great and happy consequences which we have seen that it is destined to produce. The only indispensable unity for those purposes is that of method, which can and evidently must be, and is already largely established. As to the scientific product, it is not necessary that it should be unified; it is sufficient if it be homogeneous. It is, therefore, from the double standpoint of unity of method and homogeneity of scientific propositions that the different classes of positive theories will be considered in the present work. While trying to diminish as far as possible the number of general laws necessary for the positive explanation of natural phenomena—which is the real philosophic purpose of all science—we shall think it rash ever to hope, even in the most distant future, to reduce these laws rigorously to a single one.

I have attempted in this chapter to determine, as exactly as I could, the aim, the spirit, and the influence of the positive philosophy. I have, therefore, indicated the goal toward which my labors have always tended, and always will tend unceasingly, in this course or elsewhere. No one is more profoundly convinced than myself of the inadequacy of my intellectual powers, even if they were far superior to what they are, to undertake such a vast and noble work. But, although the task is too great for a single mind or a single lifetime, yet one man can state the problem clearly, and that is all I am ambitious of doing.

Having thus expounded the true aim of this course, by setting the point of view from which I shall consider the various principal branches of natural philosophy, I shall in the next chapter complete these general preliminaries by explaining the plan I have adopted—that is to say, by determining the encyclopedic order that should be established among the several classes of natural phenomena and, consequently, among the corresponding positive sciences.

II

THE CLASSIFICATION
OF THE POSITIVE
SCIENCES

The considerations to be presented in this course on all the principal branches of natural science have been characterized as exactly as possible in the preceding chapter. We must now determine the plan that we should follow, by finding that which is the most suitable rational classification of the different fundamental positive sciences, so that we may study them in succession from the standpoint that we have adopted. This second general discussion is indispensable in order to make clear at the outset the true spirit of this course.

We can easily see in the first place that there is no need to criticize here the numerous classifications that have been successively proposed during the last two centuries as general systems of human knowledge regarded in its entirety. We are at the present time thoroughly convinced that all the encyclopedic scales—such as those of Bacon and d'Alembert[1]—which are based

---

[1] Jean le Rond d'Alembert (1717–1783). French philosopher, widely interested in the sciences, who made a special contribution to the development of dynamics in physics. A principal editor of Diderot's *Encyclopédie*.

upon any distinction between the different faculties of the human mind, are for that reason alone radically defective. That is true even when this distinction is not, as is often the case, more subtle than real; for in each of its spheres of activity our understanding makes simultaneous use of all its principal faculties. As to all the other classifications that have been proposed, it is sufficient to observe that the definite result of the different discussions raised upon this subject has been to demonstrate in each of them some radical defect or other; so that not one of them has been able to command universal assent, there being in this respect almost as many opinions as there are individuals holding them. These different attempts have, indeed, been as a rule so badly conceived that a prejudice has involuntarily arisen in most intelligent minds against every undertaking of this kind.

Without dwelling further on such a well established fact, it is more essential to seek the cause of it. We can easily account for the profound imperfection of those attempts at classification that have been renewed so often up to the present time. I need hardly say that, because of the general discredit into which works of this nature have fallen due to the inadequacy of the earlier schemes, these classifications are now seldom attempted except by persons almost entirely ignorant of the sciences which they undertake to classify. But, putting this personal consideration on one side, a much more important one, drawn from the very nature of the subject, shows clearly why it has not hitherto been possible to rise to an encyclopedic conception of a really satisfactory character. It consists in the want of homogeneity which has always existed until recently between the different parts of the intellectual system, some having successively become positive, while others remained theological or metaphysical. In such an incoherent condition of things, it was evidently impossible to establish any rational classification. How could one succeed in arranging in a single system conceptions so profoundly contradictory? It is a difficulty that necessarily proved a stumbling block to all the classifiers, and none of them were able to perceive its nature distinctly. It was very evident, however, for anyone who had grasped the true state of the human mind, that such an enterprise was premature and could not be attempted success-fully until all our principal ideas had become positive.

The explanations given in the preceding chapter show that this fundamental condition can now be regarded as fulfilled; it is therefore possible to form a truly rational and stable arrangement of a system whose parts have at last become homogeneous.

On the other hand, the general theory of classification which the philosophical labors of botanists and zoologists have estab-lished in modern times encourages us to hope for real success in such a task, for it offers us a sure guide in the true fundamental principle of the art of classifying, which had never been clearly conceived until then. This principle is a necessary consequence of the only direct application of the positive method to this ques-tion of classification, which, like every other question, should be treated as a matter of observation instead of being determined by a priori considerations. The principle is this: the classification must proceed from a direct study of the objects to be classified, and must be determined by the real affinities and natural con-nections that they present. In this way, the classification will itself become the expression of the most general fact which is manifested by a comparison in depth of the objects embraced by it.

Applying this fundamental rule to the present case, it fol-lows that the mutual dependence which actually exists between the different positive sciences must determine our classification of them; and this dependence, if it is to be real, can result only from that of the corresponding phenomena.

But before proceeding in this observational spirit to the im-portant work of classification, it is indispensable, if we are not to lose our way in a work of too great compass, that we should circumscribe more precisely than we have yet done the subject that we propose to classify.

All human works deal with either speculation or action, and the most general division of our knowledge, therefore, is into theoretical and practical. If, in the first place, we consider this primary division, it is clear that we need concern ourselves only with theoretical knowledge in a course of this kind. It is not a question of dealing with the entire system of human ideas, but only with those fundamental conceptions of the different orders of phenomena that furnish a solid basis to all our other mental combinations of whatever kind, while being themselves independent of any antecedent intellectual system. Now, in such a study it is theory that we have to consider, and not the application of it—except insofar as the application may elucidate the theory. This is probably what Bacon understood, although very imperfectly, by that "first philosophy" which he said should be extracted from the whole of the sciences, and which has been so differently, and always so strangely, conceived by the metaphysicians who have undertaken to explain his idea.

No doubt, when we embrace in our view human labor as a whole, whether theoretical or practical, we must regard our study of nature as intended to furnish us with the true rational basis for acting upon nature. For it is only by knowing the laws of phenomena, and so foreseeing their occurrence, that we are able in active life to make these phenomena modify one another for our advantage. Our direct natural power of acting upon our environment is extremely feeble and wholly disproportioned to our needs. Whenever we succeed in accomplishing anything great, it is due to the fact that our knowledge of natural laws allows us to introduce, among the fixed conditions under whose influence the different phenomena take place, some modifying elements. These, however feeble they may be in themselves, are in certain cases sufficient to turn to our advantage the final results of the sum total of external causes. We may sum up very exactly the general relation of science to art, using these two words in their widest sense, by the following very simple formula: from science comes prevision; from prevision comes action.

But, in spite of the vital importance of this relation, which must never be ignored, we should form a very imperfect idea of the sciences if we were to regard them only as the bases of the arts, an error to which our age is, unhappily, too much inclined. Immense as are the services rendered to industry by science, and although according to the striking aphorism of Bacon—knowledge is power—we must never forget that the sciences have a yet higher and more direct destination, that of satisfying the craving of our minds to know the laws of phenomena. To feel how deep and urgent this craving is, it is sufficient to reflect for a moment upon the physiological effects of astonishment, and to recollect that the most terrible sensation we can experience is that which occurs whenever any phenomenon appears to take place in violation of the natural laws that are familiar to us. This need of arranging facts in an easily comprehended order—which is the proper object of all scientific theories—is so inherent in our organization that, if we could not succeed in satisfying it by positive conceptions, we should have to return inevitably to those theological and metaphysical explanations that, as I explained in the last chapter, had their origin in this need.

I have thought it well to point out expressly at this stage a consideration that will recur frequently in the course of this work, in order to indicate the necessity of guarding against the undue influence of the habits of the present day, which tend to prevent the formation of just and noble ideas on the importance and destination of the sciences. The general tendency of our time is, in this respect, incomplete and narrow. But, in the case of scientists, it is corrected, consciously or not, by the strong natural craving of which I have spoken. Otherwise, the human intellect would be confined to researches of immediate practical utility, and, as Condorcet[2] very justly remarked, would for that reason alone be completely arrested in its progress. This would be the case even as regards those practical applications that are constantly derived from theories formed for purely scientific purposes, and that have often been cultivated during many centuries without producing any practical result. A very remarkable example of this can be cited in the beautiful speculations of the Greek geometers on conic sections. These, after a long series of generations, effected the renovation of astronomy, and so finally enabled the art of navigation to reach that degree of perfection

[2] Marie J. A. N. Caritat, Marquis de Condorcet (1743–1794) French social philosopher and radical, highly progressive in point of view, and formulator of a bold theory of historical progress.

to which it has in modern times attained, and which would never have been reached without the aid of such purely theoretical labors as those of Archimedes[3] and Apollonius.[4] This is so true that Condorcet rightly said: "The sailor who is preserved from shipwreck by an exact observation of the longitude owes his life to a theory conceived two thousand years before, by some men of genius who had in view simply geometrical speculations."

It is therefore evident that, after the study of nature has been conceived in a general way as serving for the rational basis of our action upon it, the intellect must next proceed to theoretical researches, leaving wholly on one side every practical consideration. Our means for discovering truth are so feeble that if we do not concentrate them exclusively upon this object, and if we hamper our search for truth with the extraneous condition that it shall have some immediate practical utility, it would be almost always impossible for us to succeed.

However that may be, it is certain that the aggregate of our knowledge about nature, and the aggregate of practical procedures which we deduce from that knowledge in order to modify the natural order for our advantage, form two essentially distinct systems, which it is convenient to conceive of and to cultivate separately. Besides, the first system being the base of the second, it is clearly the one that should be considered first in a methodical course of study, even if it were proposed to embrace therein the whole of human knowledge, both theoretical and practical. It appears to me that this theoretical system should be the only subject dealt with at the present day in a truly rational course of positive philosophy; at least, that is the way in which I regard the matter. No doubt it would be possible to imagine a more extended course dealing with the generalities of both

---

[3] Archimedes (ca. 287–212 B.C.). Outstanding Greek mathematician, physicist, and engineer. Responsible for theories of displacement and the lever; discoverer of fundamental geometrical principles.

[4] Apollonius of Perga (fl. 247–205 B.C.). Great Greek geometrician, especially noted for his eight-volume work on *Conic Sections*.

theory and practice. But I do not think that such an enterprise, even apart from its vast extent, could be attempted suitably in the present condition of the human mind. It seems to me, indeed, to demand previous work of a very important and wholly special nature, which has not yet been accomplished—that of constructing, in accordance with scientific theories proper, the special conceptions intended to serve as direct bases for the general operations of practice.

In the present condition of mental development, the sciences are not directly applicable to the arts, at least in the most perfect cases. Between these two orders of ideas there lies a third, which, although still ill-determined in its philosophical character, is yet very apparent when we consider the class of persons who are specially occupied with it. Between the scientists proper and the actual directors of industry an intermediate class is rising up— that of the engineers, whose particular function is to settle the relations between theory and practice. Unconcerned with the progress of scientific knowledge, they study it in its present state for the purpose of deducing from it the industrial applications that it can furnish. Such, at least, is the natural tendency of things, although there is still much confusion in this respect. The body of knowledge that should form the equipment of the engineering class and that should establish the true direct theories of the different arts, might no doubt give rise to philosophical considerations of great interest and real importance. But a work that should embrace them together with the theories founded on the pure sciences would at present be altogether premature; because these doctrines, intermediate between pure theory and direct practice, are not yet formed. Such imperfect elements of them as at present exist relate to the more advanced sciences and arts, and these merely allow us to conceive the nature and possibility of similar labors dealing with the whole body of human operations. It is thus—to cite the most important example—that we must regard the fine conception of Monge,[5] relating to descriptive geometry,

---

[5] Gaspard Monge (1746–1818). French mathematician, founder of descriptive geometry.

which is really nothing but a general theory of the arts of con-struction. Very few similar ideas have as yet been formed in other departments; I shall take care to notice them at their proper places in this course and to point out their importance. But it is clear that conceptions which up to the present are so incomplete, should not enter as an essential part into a course of positive phi-losophy, which should, as far as possible, be confined to such doc-trines as have a fixed and clearly determined character.

How difficult it is to construct these intermediate doctrines will be the better realized if we consider that every art depends not only upon a certain corresponding science, but upon several sciences simultaneously, so that the most important arts borrow direct help from almost all the different principal sciences. For example, the true theory of agriculture—to confine myself to the principal case—demands an intimate combination of physio-logical, chemical, physical, and even astronomical and mathemati-cal knowledge. The same thing is true in the case of the fine arts. Bearing this fact in mind, we easily perceive why these theories could not yet have been formed, for they assume the previous development of all the different fundamental sciences. Here, then, is another reason for not including such an order of ideas in a course of positive philosophy, since, far from being able to contribute to the systematic formation of this philosophy, the general theories peculiar to the different principal arts must, on the contrary, be a future consequence, and one of the most use-ful consequences, of its construction.

In this course, then, we must consider only scientific the-ories, and not their practical applications. But a further distinc-tion still has to be drawn with respect to the theories themselves. When this has been done, the field of our inquiry will at last be duly limited, and we shall be able to proceed to a methodical classification of the sciences with which positive philosophy is concerned.

We must distinguish, with reference to all kinds of phe-nomena, two classes of natural science. The first consists of the abstract or general sciences, whose object is the discovery of the laws regulating the different classes of phenomena in all conceivable cases. The other group comprises the concrete, special, or descriptive sciences, sometimes called the natural sciences proper, whose function consists in applying these laws to the actual history of the different existing beings. The abstract sciences are, therefore, fundamental ones, and our studies in this course are concerned with them alone; the others, whatever may be their intrinsic importance, are really only secondary sciences and, consequently, should not form part of a work whose great natural extent compels us to reduce it to the least possible development.

The distinction just drawn cannot present any difficulty to those who are at all familiar with the different positive sciences, since it is almost equivalent to the distinction which is usually made in nearly all scientific works between theoretical physics and natural history, properly so called.[6] The importance of this division of the sciences into two groups is not yet appreciated sufficiently, and some examples will serve to render its nature more evident.

The distinction may, in the first place, be perceived very clearly by comparing, on the one hand, general physiology, and on the other, zoology and botany. Studying the laws of life in general, and determining the mode of existence of each living being as an individual, are evidently two works of very different character. The second study is, besides, necessarily founded on the first.

The same thing is true in the case of chemistry as contrasted with mineralogy; the first science is evidently the rational basis of the second one. In chemistry we consider every possible molecular combination in every imaginable circumstance; in mineralogy we consider only those combinations that are actually found to occur as constituents of the earth and as subject to terrestrial influences alone. The difference between the chemical and the mineralogical standpoint, although both sciences deal

6 Compare Stephen Toulmin, *The Philosophy of Science: An Introduction* (New York: Harper Torchbooks, 1960), for a contemporary discussion that makes much fruitful use of this basic distinction.

with the same objects, is clearly shown by the circumstance that the majority of the facts considered in chemistry have only an artificial existence; so that a body such as chlorine or potassium may possess great chemical importance owing to the extent and energy of its affinities, whereas its mineralogical interest may be almost nil. On the other hand, although a mineralogist would have a great deal to say about a compound such as granite or quartz, such a substance would be of little interest from a chemist's standpoint.

What makes still more evident the logical necessity of this fundamental distinction between the two great sections of natural philosophy is the fact that not only does each section of concrete physics presuppose the previous study of the corresponding section of abstract physics, but it also demands a knowledge of the general laws relative to all orders of phenomena. Thus, for example, the special study of the earth, considered under every possible aspect, not only demands a previous acquaintance with physics and chemistry, but it cannot be accomplished properly without introducing, on the one hand, astronomical, and, on the other hand, physiological, knowledge; so that geology is related to the entire system of fundamental sciences. The same thing is true of each of the other concrete sciences. It is precisely for this reason that concrete physics has up to the present made so little real progress, because its study could not be begun in a truly rational manner until all the different principal branches of abstract physics had acquired a definite character, which did not occur until our own time. Until that had taken place, it was possible to collect upon this subject only some more or less uncoordinated materials, which are still very incomplete. The known facts cannot be coordinated in such a way as to form true special theories of the different beings of the universe until the fundamental distinction between the abstract and concrete sciences is more profoundly felt and more regularly organized, and until the scientists who are specially devoted to the study of the concrete sciences recognize the necessity of founding their researches upon a knowledge in depth of all the fundamental abstract sciences. The latter is a condition that is still very far from being fulfilled properly at the present day.

Examining this condition, we find a confirmatory reason why, in this course of positive philosophy, we should confine ourselves to considering the abstract or general sciences, and not include at the same time the descriptive or special sciences. Here it comes to light that a new essential property of the study of the generalities of abstract physics is to furnish the rational basis of a truly systematic concrete physics. In the present condition of human intelligence there would, therefore, be a species of contradiction in wishing to unite the two orders of science in a single course. We can say, moreover, that, even if concrete physics had already attained the same degree of perfection as abstract physics, so that it would be possible consequently to embrace both at the same time in a course of positive philosophy, it evidently would be nonetheless necessary to commence with the abstract section, for that would remain the invariable base of the other. It is clear, besides, that the study of the generalities alone of the fundamental sciences is so extensive by itself that it is important to set aside as much as possible all considerations that are not indispensable; now, those relating to the secondary sciences will always be in any case of a distinct order. Since the philosophy of the fundamental sciences presents a system of positive conceptions upon all the categories of real knowledge, it is for that reason alone sufficient to constitute that "first philosophy" which Bacon sought; and, since it is destined henceforth to serve as the permanent basis for all human speculations, it should be carefully reduced to the simplest possible expression.

I need not pursue this argument further at present, for I shall have several opportunities of recurring to it in the different parts of this course. I have said enough to explain how and why I limit our inquiry.

It follows, then, from the considerations that have been set forth in this chapter: (1) that human knowledge as a whole being composed of theoretical and of practical knowledge, we are concerned here only with the former; (2) that theoretical knowledge, or science, properly so called, being divided into general and special sciences, we have only to consider here the first kind, and, as interesting as concrete physics may be, it is to abstract physics that we must confine ourselves.

The proper subject of this course having thus been exactly limited, it is now easy to proceed to a really satisfactory rational classification of the fundamental sciences, which is the encyclopedic question forming the special subject of this chapter.

We must in the first place recognize that, however natural such a classification may be, it necessarily always involves something, if not arbitrary, at least artificial. Inevitably, therefore, it will be imperfect.

The principal object to be kept in view in every attempt at classification is the arrangement of the sciences in the order of their natural connection, according to their mutual dependence, so that one might be able to present them successively, without ever being in the smallest degree involved in a vicious circle. Now, that is a condition that seems to me impossible to fulfill quite rigorously. Perhaps I may be allowed here to develop this reflection at some length; it is in my opinion an important one, for herein lies the real difficulty of the present inquiry. Besides, its treatment will give me an opportunity of establishing, in connection with the exposition of our knowledge, a general principle that I shall have to apply frequently later on.

It is this. Every science can be expounded according to two essentially distinct methods—the historical and the theoretical; every other mode of exposition is only a combination of these methods.

By the first method, the knowledge is presented in the same order as that in which the human mind actually obtained it, following as far as possible the actual track pursued.

By the second method, the system of ideas is presented as it might be conceived of today by a single mind which, being placed at the right point of view and furnished with sufficient knowledge, should apply itself to the reconstruction of the science as a whole.

The first mode is evidently that by which the study of every new science must of necessity commence, because it presents the feature of not requiring for the exposition of the knowledge any new independent work. The didactic art reduces itself in that case to the studying in chronological order of the different original works that have contributed to the progress of the science. The theoretical method supposes, on the contrary, that all these individual works have been recast into a general system, so that they may be presented in a more natural logical order; it is, therefore, applicable only to a science that has already arrived at a sufficiently high degree of development. But in proportion as the science progresses, the historical order of exposition becomes more and more impracticable, owing to the lengthy series of intermediate works that the mind would be compelled to survey; whereas the theoretical order becomes more and more possible, and at the same time necessary, because new conceptions permit the earlier discoveries to be presented under a more direct point of view.

The education of an ancient geometer, for example, consisted simply in studying, in due order, the very small number of original treatises on the different parts of geometry which then existed; and this amounted to little more than the writings of Archimedes and Apollonius.[7] On the other hand, a modern geometer has usually finished his education without having read a single original work, except in the case of the most recent discoveries which can be known only by this means.

The constant tendency of the human mind in the exposition of its knowledge is, therefore, to substitute more and more the theoretical for the historical method, the former alone being suited to the mature state of our intelligence.

The general problem of intellectual education consists in enabling an individual of usually but average ability to reach in a few years the same stage of development that has been attained during a long series of ages by the efforts of a large number of superior thinkers, who have throughout their lives concentrated their attention upon the same subject. It is accordingly clear that, although it is infinitely easier and quicker to learn than to originate, it would be quite impossible to attain the desired end if we tried to compel each individual mind to pass successively through the same intermediate stages that the collective genius of man-

[7] See notes 3 and 4, p. 40.

kind has necessarily had to traverse. Hence, the indispensable need for the theoretical method, as is especially evident at the present day in the most advanced sciences, the ordinary teaching of which shows hardly any trace of the actual steps of their evolution.

We must add, however, in order to avoid any exaggeration, that every actual mode of teaching in use is necessarily a certain combination of the theoretical and historical orders; all that the former can claim is a constant and increasing predominance. The theoretical order cannot, indeed, be followed quite rigorously, for, as we have seen, it implies that the scientific truths have been not only discovered, but systematically recast. Now, such recasting will not at any given time embrace the truths most recently discovered. These, therefore, can be taught only according to the historical arrangement, which will not in such cases be attended with the chief inconveniences that prevent its general adoption.

The only fundamental objection that can be urged against the theoretical method is that it leaves the student in ignorance of the way in which the different sciences have been built-up; a question that, although distinct from the actual acquisition of these sciences, is in itself of the highest interest for every philosophical mind. This consideration would, in my opinion, have much weight if it were really an argument in favor of the historical order. But it is evident that learning the truths of a science in their historical order, and learning the actual history of that science, are two quite different studies, as I shall now show.

The different subdivisions of each science, which we are led to separate in the theoretical order, are in reality developed simultaneously and under the mutual influence of each other. That is a fact which would naturally tend to make us prefer the historical order. But when we consider in its entirety the actual development of the human mind, we see further that the different sciences themselves have, in fact, received improvement simultaneously and from one another. We even see that there is an interdependence between the progress of the sciences and that of the arts, owing to their innumerable reciprocal influences, and, finally, that they have all been closely connected with the general development of human society. This vast interlacement is so real that, in order to understand how a scientific theory actually arose, it is often necessary to consider the improvement in some art that has no rational link with it, or even some particular progress in social organization without which this discovery could never have taken place. We shall see numerous examples of this as we proceed. It follows from that which has been said that we can know only the true history of each science—that is to say, the way in which the discoveries composing it were actually made—by making a direct study of the general history of humanity. That is the reason why all the documents hitherto collected on the history of mathematics, astronomy, medicine, etc., however precious they may be, can be regarded only as materials for the work.

The professedly historical order of exposition, even if it could be rigorously followed as regards the details of each particular science, would still be purely hypothetical and abstract under the most important aspect, for it would consider the development of the science as though it had been an isolated thing. Far from exhibiting the true history of the science, it would lead to a very false conception of it.

We are certainly convinced that a knowledge of the history of the sciences is of the highest importance, and I even think that a science is not completely known if we are ignorant of its history. But this historical study of the sciences should be looked upon as entirely separate from its proper and theoretical study, without which, indeed, the history would not be intelligible. I shall, therefore, consider carefully the true history of the fundamental sciences which are to be the subject of our inquiries; but I shall do so only in the last part of this course—that relating to the study of social phenomena—in treating of the general development of humanity, of which the history of the sciences constitutes the most important, although hitherto the most neglected, part. In the study of each science, such incidental historical considerations as may present themselves will have a clearly distinct character, so as not to affect the proper nature of our principal study.

The preceding discussion which, as we see, must be specially developed later on, tends to define more precisely the true spirit of this course by presenting it under a new point of view. But its chief bearing on the question immediately before us is that it determines exactly the conditions that we must accept and that we can justly hope to fulfill, in constructing an encyclopedic scale of the different fundamental sciences.

Indeed, we see that, however perfect we might suppose it to be, this classification can never absolutely conform to the historical succession of the sciences. Do what we may, we cannot avoid entirely the necessity of presenting as of an earlier date a science that, under some more or less important special aspects, may, however, need to borrow from the ideas of another science of subsequent rank. But we must take care to avoid such derangements with respect to the characteristic conceptions of each science, for in that case the classification would be entirely defective.

Thus, for example, it appears to me unquestionable that in the general system of the sciences, astronomy should be placed before physics, properly so called; and yet, several branches of physics, especially optics, are indispensable to the complete exposition of astronomy.

Minor defects of this kind, which are strictly inevitable, cannot invalidate a classification that in other respects suitably fulfils the principal conditions of the case. They are due to the necessarily artificial element in our division of intellectual work.

Nevertheless, although for the reasons already given it would have been improper to take the historical order for the basis of our classification, I claim as an essential quality of the encyclopedic scale, which I am going to propose, that it does broadly accord with the whole history of science. By this I mean that, in spite of the real and continuous simultaneity of development of the different sciences, those which will be classed as anterior did, as a matter of fact, start earlier and always continued to be more advanced than those classed as posterior to them. This is what should inevitably occur if we take—as clearly we ought to—the natural logical connection of the sciences for our principle of classification, the starting point of mankind having necessarily been the same as that of the individual.

The exact difficulty of this question of the classification of the sciences is well illustrated by a very simple mathematical consideration, which will also serve to sum up all the previous arguments in this chapter.

The problem before us is the classification of the fundamental sciences. We shall soon see that, all things considered, it is not possible to distinguish less than six of these; most scientists would very likely admit a much larger number. That point settled, we know that six objects permit of 720 distinct classifications. The fundamental sciences could, therefore, give rise to 720 different classifications, among which we have to choose the one classification that best satisfies the principal conditions of the problem. We see that, in spite of the great number of encyclopedic scales successively proposed up to the present, the discussion has as yet been confined to a very small number of the possible arrangements. Nevertheless, I believe we can say without any exaggeration that, on examining each of the 720 classifications, there would not perhaps be a single one in favor of which we could not find some plausible arguments. On observing the different arrangements that have been actually proposed, we remark the most extreme differences among them, sciences that are placed by some at the head of the encyclopedic system being referred by others to the opposite extremity, and vice versa. The real difficulty of the question before us consists, then, in choosing the one truly rational order out of the very considerable number of possible systems.

Approaching this great question now in a direct manner, we must in the first place remember that, in order to obtain a natural and positive classification of the fundamental sciences, we must seek its principle in the comparison of the various orders of phenomena, the discovery of whose laws is the object of those sciences. What we want to determine is the real dependence of the different scientific studies. Now, this dependence can result only from that of the corresponding phenomena.

By considering all observable phenomena under this aspect, we shall presently see that it is possible to class them in a small number of natural categories, so arranged that the rational study of each category may be founded on a knowledge of the principal laws of the preceding one while serving as the basis of the following one. This order is determined by the degree of simplicity, or, that which comes to the same thing, of generality of the phenomena. Hence results their successive dependence and, consequently, the greater or lesser facility in their study.

It is clear, indeed a priori, that the simplest phenomena— those which are least complicated by others—are necessarily also the most general; for whatever is observed in the greatest number of cases is for that reason disengaged to the utmost degree from the circumstances peculiar to each separate case. We must, therefore, begin with the study of the most general or simple phenomena, proceeding from them successively to the most special or complex. This is necessary if we wish to comprehend natural philosophy in a really methodical manner; because this order of generality or simplicity, while it necessarily determines the rational connection of the several fundamental sciences by the successive dependence of their phenomena, at the same time fixes the degree of facility in their study.

There is also a secondary consideration which is, I think, important to notice here, and it leads to exactly the same conclusion as the preceding arguments. The most general or simple phenomena, being of necessity the farthest removed from the human order, must, consequently, admit of being studied in a calmer and more rational frame of mind; that, then, is a further reason why the corresponding sciences have been developed more rapidly.

Having thus indicated the fundamental rule that must preside over the classification of the sciences, I can now proceed immediately to the construction of the encyclopedic scale, according to which the plan of this course must be determined, and which each reader will easily be able to appreciate with the aid of the preceding considerations.

A first glance at the aggregate of natural phenomena leads us to divide them at a start—in accordance with the principle we have just established—into two great principal classes: the first comprises all the phenomena of inorganic bodies; the second, all those of organic bodies.

The latter are evidently more complex and less general than

the others; they depend upon the inorganic, which, on the contrary, are in no way dependent upon the organic. Hence arises the necessity of not studying physiological phenomena until the phenomena of inorganic bodies have been considered. In whatever way we may explain the differences between these two kinds of beings, it is certain that we observe in living bodies all the phenomena, whether mechanical or chemical, which occur in inorganic bodies, with the addition of a wholly special order of phenomena, the vital phenomena, properly so called, which belong to organization. There is no need to ask if the two classes of bodies are, or are not, of the same nature—that is an insoluble question which is still too much debated in our time owing to the lingering influence of theological and metaphysical habits. Such a question does not enter into the domain of the positive philosophy, which formally declares its absolute ignorance as to the ultimate nature of any body whatsoever. But it is by no means indispensable to look upon inorganic and living bodies as of essentially different natures, in order to recognize the necessity of separating the two studies.

No doubt, there is not yet sufficient agreement upon the general mode of regarding the phenomena of living bodies. But, whatever view may come to be adopted owing to the future progress of natural philosophy, the classification which we are establishing will not in any way be affected by that. Indeed, if we could regard as demonstrated, the idea for which the present state of physiology affords hardly any justification—that physiological phenomena are always simply mechanical, electrical, and chemical phenomena modified by the structure and composition proper to organized bodies—our fundamental division would nonetheless hold good. For it still remains true, even in this case, that we should study general phenomena before proceeding to the examination of the special modifications that they undergo in certain *entities* of the universe owing to a peculiar arrangement of their molecules. Most enlightened minds at the present day base this division upon the diversity of the laws concerned; but it is necessarily a permanent one on account of the subordination of the phenomena and, consequently, of the sciences dealing with them, whatever affinity the future may establish between these two classes of bodies.

This is not the place to develop in detail a general comparison between inorganic and living bodies, because that will be the special subject of a thorough examination in the physiological section of this work. It is sufficient for the present to have recognized in principle the logical necessity of separating from each other the sciences relating to these classes of phenomena, and of not proceeding to the study of "organic physics" until we have established the general laws of inorganic physics.

Each of these two great halves of natural philosophy can be subdivided into two branches. We obtain them by a further application of the same general rule.

Take, first, inorganic physics. Following, as before, the order of the generality and dependence of the phenomena, we see in the first place that it must be divided into two distinct sections, according to the manner in which it deals with phenomena general to the universe or those special to terrestrial bodies. Hence, we have celestial physics, or astronomy (whether geometrical or mechanical), and terrestrial physics. The necessity for the division is exactly the same as that for the division into organic and inorganic.

Astronomical phenomena being the most general, simple, and abstract of all, the study of natural philosophy must evidently begin with them; for the laws of astronomy influence those of all other phenomena, but the laws of other phenomena do not influence those of astronomy. All the phenomena of terrestrial physics present the general effect of universal gravitation; they present, in addition, other effects peculiar to themselves and modifying those of gravitation. Hence, if we analyze the simplest terrestrial phenomenon—it need not be a chemical, it may be a purely mechanical one—we always find it to be more complex than the most complicated celestial phenomenon. The most difficult astronomical question, therefore, really presents a less complicated subject for investigation, if all the determining circumstances be taken into account, than the simple movement of a heavy body, even if it be only a solid. Such a consideration shows clearly how indispensable it is to separate distinctly celestial from terrestrial physics, and only to proceed to the study of the first which forms its rational basis.

Terrestrial physics is, in its turn, subdivided in the same manner into two very distinct portions, according to the way in which we regard bodies from the mechanical or chemical standpoint. Hence we have physics proper and chemistry. The latter, if it is to be considered in a truly logical manner, evidently presupposes a previous acquaintance with physics. For all chemical phenomena are necessarily more complicated than physical ones; they depend on the physical phenomena without influencing them in return. Everyone knows, in fact, that all chemical action is in the first place subject to the influence of weight, height, electricity, etc.; and it presents, in addition, something peculiar to itself which modifies the action of the preceding agents. This consideration, while it exhibits chemistry as necessarily following after physics, at the same time presents it as a distinct science. For whatever opinion we may adopt regarding chemical affinity, and even if we should see in it—as is conceivable—only mere modifications of general gravitation produced by the form and mutual arrangement of the atoms, it would still remain unquestionable that the necessity of continually taking these special conditions into account would not allow of our treating chemistry as a simple appendage to physics. We should, therefore, in any case, be compelled, if only to facilitate our studies, to maintain that division and order of succession which are regarded now as due to the heterogeneity of the phenomena.

Such, then, is the rational distribution of the principal branches of the general science of inorganic bodies. An analogous division arises in the same manner in the general science of organic bodies.

All living beings present two essentially distinct orders of phenomena—those which relate to the individual, and those which concern the species, especially when it is sociable. It is principally with regard to man that this distinction is fundamental. The last order of phenomena is evidently more complex and special than the first; it depends on the first without influencing it in return. Hence, we have two great sections in "organic physics"—physiology, properly so called, and social physics, which is based upon it.

In all social phenomena we perceive in the first place the influence of the physiological laws of the individual, and, in addition, something which modifies their effect arising from the action of the individuals upon each other—singularly complicated in the case of the human race by the action of each generation on its successor. It is, therefore, evident that, in order to study social phenomena properly, we must start with a good knowledge of the laws relating to the life of the individual. On the other hand, the necessary subordination between the two studies does not oblige us to regard social physics as a mere appendage of physiology, as some eminent physiologists have been led to believe. Although the phenomena are certainly homogeneous, they are not identical, and the separation of the two sciences is of the highest importance. It would be impossible to treat the collective study of the species as a pure deduction from the study of the individual, for the social conditions which modify the action of the physiological laws are here the most essential consideration. Social physics must, therefore, be founded on a set of direct observations peculiar to itself; due regard always being paid to its necessarily intimate relationship with physiology proper.

If we wanted our classification to be perfectly symmetrical, we could easily make a further subdivision of "organic physics," as we have already made of inorganic, by availing ourselves of the usual division of physiology proper into vegetable and animal. Such a division would be based on the principle of classification already employed, for the phenomena of animal life are, for the most part, more complex and special than those of vegetable life. But the endeavor to obtain such exact symmetry would be puerile if it involved ignoring or exaggerating the real analogies or actual differences between phenomena. Now, it is certain that the distinction between vegetable and animal physiology, although of great importance in that which I have called concrete physics, has hardly any significance in abstract physics, which alone concerns us here. The knowledge of the general laws of life, which we should look upon as the true object of physiology, requires the simultaneous consideration of the entire organic series without any distinction between plant and animal —a distinction that is, moreover, daily fading away in proportion as those phenomena are studied more deeply.

We shall continue, therefore, to consider that there is only a single division in "organic physics," although we have thought it necessary to establish two successive ones in inorganic physics.

It follows from the foregoing discussion that the positive philosophy is naturally divided into five fundamental sciences, whose succession is determined by a necessary and invariable subordination, founded merely on a thorough comparison of the corresponding phenomena—quite apart from any hypothetical view on the subject. These sciences are: astronomy, physics, chemistry, physiology, and, lastly, social physics. The first considers the most general, simple, and abstract phenomena—those which are most remote from human interests; they affect all other phenomena, without in turn being influenced by them. The phenomena considered by the last science are, on the contrary, the most special, complicated, and concrete phenomena—those which most directly concern human interests; they depend more or less upon all the preceding phenomena without, however, exercizing any influence upon them. Between these two extremes, the degrees of speciality, complexity, and individuality of the phenomena continue gradually to augment in the same proportion as their successive dependence. Such is the most essential general relationship between the different fundamental sciences. We have arrived at it, not by drawing arbitrary and empty distinctions, but by a proper use of true philosophic observation. Such must, therefore, be the plan of this course.

I have been able here only to set forth in outline the principal considerations on which this classification rests. To comprehend it thoroughly, it would now be necessary, having viewed it from a general standpoint, to examine it in its special relationship to each fundamental science. We shall do that carefully on commencing the special study of each part of this course. The revision of the encyclopedic scale, undertaken in this way at the commencement of each of the five great sciences, should make the scale itself more exact and its soundness more evident. The advantages of this plan will be all the clearer because we shall then see the subdivisions of each science falling naturally into order according to the same principle; so that we shall have the whole system of human knowledge analyzed, even in its secondary details, in accordance with a rule applied universally—that of the degree of abstraction of the corresponding conceptions. But studies of this kind, besides taking us much too far now, would certainly be out of place in this chapter, where we should maintain our thoughts at the most general standpoint of the positive philosophy.

Nevertheless, as I shall be constantly employing this fundamental classification throughout the present course, I wish from the outset to make its importance understood. I will, therefore, rapidly review here its most essential general properties.

In the first place, a very decisive confirmation of its accuracy is afforded by the circumstance that it is in substantial conformity with the kind of spontaneous arrangement that is, in fact, virtually admitted by scientific specialists.

Framers of encyclopedic scales usually take no pains to treat as distinct those sciences which, in the actual course of intellectual progress and without any premeditated design, have been cultivated separately, or to coordinate them in conformity with the real relations exhibited in their daily development. Yet, such an accord is evidently the surest index of a good classification; because the divisions that have been introduced spontaneously into the scientific system can have been due only to a long-experienced feeling of the true needs of the human mind, a feeling that had arisen at a time when there was no erroneous theorizing to lead people astray.

But although the classification proposed above fulfills this condition entirely—a fact that it would be superfluous to prove —we must not, therefore, conclude that the habits generally established at the present day among scientists, as the result of experience, would make the work of classification which I have just performed unnecessary. They have only rendered such an operation possible, for there is a fundamental difference between an arrangement reached only empirically and the same arrangement conceived rationally. Furthermore, this classification is not usually conceived—still less employed—with all the needful precision, nor is its importance properly appreciated; a sufficient proof of that is the serious breaches of this encyclopedic law which are committed every day to the great detriment of the human intellect.

A second very essential character of our classification is that it necessarily conforms to the actual order of development of natural philosophy. This fact is verified by all that we know of the history of the sciences, especially in the last two centuries, during which we can follow their progress with much greater accuracy.

We see, in fact, that the rational study of each fundamental science demanded the previous study of all those that preceded it in our encyclopedic scale; it could not, therefore, make any real progress and acquire its true character until there had been a considerable development of the earlier sciences, dealing with phenomena more general and more abstract, but less complex, and not dependent on those later than themselves. It is, therefore, in this order that the progress, although simultaneous, was bound to take place.

This consideration seems to me so important that I do not think it is possible really to understand the history of the human mind without paying regard to it. The general law of the three stages, which governs the whole of this history, and which was explained in the preceding chapter,[8] cannot be understood properly unless it be applied in combination with the encyclopedic formula just established. For it is according to the order enunciated by this formula that the different human theories have successively attained, first, the theological; then, the metaphysical; and, finally, the positive, state. If, in applying the law, we do not bear in mind this necessary progression, we shall often

[8] See above, pp. 1–24.

encounter difficulties which will appear insurmountable. It is clear that the theological or metaphysical state of certain fundamental theories was bound to coincide for a time, and, as a matter of fact, has at times coincided, with the positive state of others that precede them in our encyclopedic system. To verify the fundamental law of filiation would, therefore, be difficult, did we not at the same time take into account the complementary law of classification.

In the third place, this classification presents the very remarkable property of indicating in a precise manner the relative perfection of the different sciences. They approach perfection in proportion as their truths are more precisely known and completely coordinated.

It is easy to see, indeed, that the more general, simple, and abstract any phenomena are, the less they depend on others and the more precise the sciences concerned with them become, while at the same time their coordination admits of greater perfection. Thus, organic phenomena do not permit of such an exact and systematic study as the phenomena of inorganic bodies. In the same way, in inorganic physics we see that celestial phenomena, because of their much greater generality and their independence of all other phenomena, have given rise to a much more precise and closely connected science than terrestrial physics.

This fact, which is such a striking one in the actual study of the sciences, and has often given rise to chimerical hopes or unjust comparisons, is then completely explained by the encyclopedic order now established. I shall naturally have occasion to give it its full extension in the next chapter, when I shall show that the possibility of applying mathematical analysis to the study of different phenomena, and so obtaining for such study the highest possible degree of precision and coordination, is in exact proportion to the rank that these phenomena occupy in my encyclopedic scale.

I must here put the reader on his guard against a very serious error, which, although gross, is still extremely common. It consists in confounding the degree of precision of which the different sciences admit with their degree of certitude, whence results the very dangerous assumption that, because the first is obviously very unequal, the second must be so also. Thus, people still often speak, although less than formerly, of the unequal certainty of the different sciences, which tends to discourage directly the cultivation of the most difficult ones. It is clear, nevertheless, that precision and certainty are two qualities of very different nature. A wholly absurd proposition may be very precise, as if we should say, for example, that the sum of the angles of a triangle is equal to three right angles; and a very certain proposition may admit only of very imperfect precision as, for instance, when we affirm that every man will die. If, as the preceding explanation shows, the different sciences must necessarily exhibit a very unequal degree of precision, that is by no means the case as regards their certitude. Each can offer results as certain as those of any other science, provided that its conclusions are not pushed beyond the degree of precision of which the corresponding phenomena admit, a condition that may not be always very easy to fulfill. In any science whatever, everything that is simply conjectural is only more or less probable, and it is not that which constitutes its essential domain; everything that is positive—that is to say, founded on well established facts—is certain, and there is not any distinction between the sciences in this respect.

Finally, the most interesting property of our encyclopedic formula—because of the importance and multiplicity of the immediate applications that can be made of it—is to determine directly the true general plan of an entirely rational scientific education. That follows immediately from the mere composition of the formula.

It is, indeed, evident that, before undertaking the methodical study of any of the fundamental sciences, it is necessary to prepare oneself by the examination of the sciences preceding it in our encyclopedic scale. The reason for this is that the earlier sciences always have a preponderating influence upon the later ones. This consideration is so striking that, notwithstanding its extreme practical importance, I have no need to insist further just now upon a principle which, moreover, will inevitably recur later in relation to each fundamental science. I will confine myself to the remark that, if it is eminently applicable to general education, it is particularly so to the special education of scientists.

Thus, physicists who have not first studied astronomy, at least under its general aspect; chemists who, before applying themselves to their special science, have not previously studied astronomy and then physics; physiologists who have not prepared themselves for their special labors by a preliminary study of astronomy, physics, and chemistry—all these lack one of the fundamental conditions of their intellectual development. This is still more evident in the case of students who wish to devote themselves to the positive study of social phenomena, without having acquired in the first place a general knowledge of astronomy, physics, chemistry, and physiology.

Because these conditions are very rarely fulfilled at present, and because no regular institution has been organized to carry them out, we must acknowledge that no truly rational education yet exists for scientists. This consideration is, in my opinion, of such great importance that I do not hesitate to attribute in part to this defect in our present educational system the state of extreme imperfection that we still witness in the more difficult sciences—a state of imperfection far out of proportion to that which is required even by the great complexity of the phenomena involved.

As regards general education, this condition is still more necessary. I regard it as so indispensable that I believe instruction in the sciences will fail to effect its most important general result in society—the renovation of our entire intellectual system—unless those sciences are studied in their proper order. We must not forget that in almost all minds, even the highest, ideas usually remain associated together according to the order in which they were first acquired; and it is, consequently, in most cases an irremediable evil not to have commenced at the beginning. The number of persons in any century who, after arriving at manhood, are able, like Bacon, Descartes, and Leibniz,[9] to make a

[9] Gottfried Wilhelm von Leibniz (1646–1716). German philosopher and mathematician, a universal genius of first rank.

clean sweep of their acquired ideas and reconstruct them systematically from the foundation is small indeed.

The importance of our encyclopedic law as a basis for scientific education can only be appreciated properly by considering it also in relation to method, instead of regarding it only as we have hitherto done, from the standpoint of theoretical content.

Under this new aspect, the carrying out of the general plan of education which we have laid down must have as its necessary result the acquisition of a perfect knowledge of the positive method, which could not be obtained in any other manner.

For natural phenomena have been classed in such a way that those which are really homogeneous always remain comprised within the same science, whereas those which belong to different sciences are really heterogeneous. The consequence is that the general positive method will be constantly modified in a uniform manner throughout the extent of each fundamental science; and it will be continually undergoing different modifications of increasing complexity in passing from one science to another. In this way we shall be certain of having considered all the real modifications of which it admits. We should have no such certainty if we adopted an encyclopedic formula that did not fulfill the essential conditions laid down above.

This new consideration is of truly fundamental importance. As we saw in a general way in the last chapter, it is impossible to understand the positive method apart from its application, and we must add further that we can form a clear and exact idea of it only by studying successively in due order its application to all the different principal classes of natural phenomena. No one science, however well chosen, would be sufficient for the attainment of this object. Of course, the method is essentially the same in all. But it has various forms of procedure, each of which is specially developed in some one science, and being less developed in the others would in them escape notice. Thus, for instance, the principal means of exploration in some sciences is observation, properly so called; in others it is experiment, and a particular kind of experiment. Similarly, we notice that this or that general precept, forming an integral part of the scientific method, was originally suggested by some particular science; and, although it may have been applied subsequently in others, it is at its original source that we must study it if we would know it thoroughly; for example, the theory of classification is best studied in biology.

If we limited ourselves to the study of a single science, we should no doubt choose the most perfect one in order to obtain the best idea of the positive method. But, as the most perfect is at the same time the simplest, we should in this way obtain only a very incomplete knowledge of the method, for we should not learn what essential modifications it must undergo in order to adapt it to more complex phenomena. Each fundamental science has in this respect, therefore, some advantages which are peculiar to it. This clearly shows the necessity of paying regard to all of them, lest we should form too narrow conceptions and inadequate mental habits. As this consideration will recur frequently in the course of the work, it is unnecessary to develop it further at this stage.

I must, nevertheless, insist here specially, with a view to a sound knowledge of the method, on the need not only of studying all the fundamental sciences in a philosophical manner, but of studying them according to the encyclopedic order established in this chapter. How can a mind, unless of the highest natural superiority, produce anything rational if it begins by studying the most complex phenomena without having previously learned to know, by examining simpler phenomena, what a law is, what it is to observe, what a positive conception is, and even what a connected argument is? Such, however, is still at the present day the ordinary procedure with our young physiologists, who plunge immediately into the study of living bodies, without as a rule any preparation other than the study of one or two dead languages, with at most only a very superficial knowledge of physics and chemistry. The latter knowledge is almost valueless from the standpoint of method, for it has not usually been obtained in a rational manner, nor by starting from the true point of departure in natural philosophy. We can see how important it is to reform such a defective course of study. In the same way, with regard to social phenomena, which are still more complicated, would it not be taking an important step toward the return of modern society to a truly normal state, if we recognized the logical necessity of not proceeding to the study of these phenomena until the mind of the student had been gradually trained by a philosophical examination of all the preceding phenomena? It would be quite true to say that this constitutes the principal difficulty, for there are few able minds at the present day which are not convinced that we must study social phenomena according to the positive method. But those who are engaged in this study do not, and cannot, know exactly in what this method consists, because they have not examined it in its earlier applications. This maxim has, therefore, up to the present remained barren as regards the renovation of social theories which have not yet emerged from the theological or metaphysical state, in spite of the efforts of so-called positive reformers. Later on this consideration will be treated in full; at present I must confine myself to pointing it out, so as to show the whole scope of the encyclopedic conception that has been propounded in this chapter.

Such, then, are the four principal aspects under which I have thought it necessary to exhibit the general importance of the rational and positive classification of the fundamental sciences.

In order to complete the general explanation of the plan of this course, I have now to consider an immense and all important gap which has been intentionally left in my encyclopedic formula; it is an omission which the reader has no doubt already noticed. I refer to the fact that we have not yet found a place for mathematics in our scientific system.

It is just because of its importance that I have not yet mentioned this great and fundamental science. The next chapter will be devoted entirely to the exact determination of its true general character, and, consequently, of its encyclopedic rank. But, in order not to leave such a serious blank in the great plan that I have tried to sketch out in this chapter, a summary account must be given here of the general results of the examination that we shall undertake in the following chapter.

In the present state of development of our positive knowledge we must, I think, look upon mathematics, not so much as a constituent part of natural philosophy, properly so called, but as having been, since Descartes and Newton, the true fundamental basis of the whole of that philosophy; although it is, strictly speaking, both one and the other. At the present time, indeed, mathematical science is of much less importance for the knowledge in which it consists—real and valuable as that knowledge is—than for constituting the most powerful instrument that the human mind can employ in investigating the laws of natural phenomena.

To form in this respect a perfectly clear and rigorously exact conception of mathematics, we see that it must be divided into two great sciences whose character is essentially distinct: abstract mathematics, or the calculus—using that word in its widest sense—and concrete mathematics, which is composed of general geometry and rational mechanics. The concrete part is founded necessarily on the abstract part, and it becomes in its turn the direct basis of all natural philosophy, all the phenomena of the universe being regarded as far as possible as either geometrical or mechanical.

The abstract part is the only portion that is purely instrumental, being simply an immense and admirable extension of natural logic to a certain order of deductions. Geometry and mechanics must, on the contrary, be regarded as true natural sciences, founded like all others on observation; although, because of the extreme simplicity of their phenomena, they admit of an infinitely more perfect degree of systematization, which has sometimes led to the experimental character of their first principles being too often neglected. But these two principal sciences possess this peculiarity—that in the present state of the human mind they are already, and will be more and more, employed as method rather than as direct doctrine.

It is also evident that, in thus placing mathematical science at the head of positive philosophy, we are making only a further application of the same principle of classification that has furnished us with the encyclopedic series established in this chapter—a principle founded on the successive dependence of the sciences, which results from the more or less abstract character of the phenomena with which they deal. We are now only restoring to this series its true first term, the peculiar importance of which demanded a special and fuller examination. We see, in fact, that geometrical and mechanical phenomena are the most general, simple, abstract, and irreducible of all, and that they do not depend on the others, but, on the contrary, are their basis. We also see that their study is an indispensable preliminary to that of all the other orders of phenomena. It is, therefore, mathematical science that must constitute the true starting point of all rational scientific education, whether general or special. This explains the universal custom that for a long while has been established on this subject in an empirical manner, although it had no origin other than the greater relative antiquity of mathematics. I must confine myself for the present to this very rapid sketch of these different considerations.

In this chapter, then, we have determined exactly the rational plan that should constantly guide us in the study of positive philosophy, not deducing it from vague arbitrary speculations, but regarding the question as the subject of a true philosophical problem. As the final result we have mathematics, astronomy, physics, chemistry, physiology, and social physics. That is the encyclopedic formula which, among the numerous possible classifications of the six fundamental sciences, is the only one conforming logically to the natural and invariable order of phenomena.

INDEX